Mastering High Performance with Kotlin

Overcome performance difficulties in Kotlin with a range of exciting techniques and solutions

Igor Kucherenko

BIRMINGHAM - MUMBAI

Mastering High Performance with Kotlin

Commissioning Editor: Richa Tripathi
Acquisition Editor: Sandeep Mishra
Content Development Editor: Zeeyan Pinheiro
Technical Editor: Ruvika Rao
Copy Editor: Safis Editing
Project Coordinator: Vaidehi Sawant
Proofreader: Safis Editing
Indexer: Tejal Daruwale Soni
Graphics: Jason Monteiro
Production Coordinator: Shraddha Falebhai

First published: June 2018

Production reference: 1120618

Published by Packt Publishing Ltd.
Livery Place
35 Livery Street
Birmingham
B3 2PB, UK.

ISBN 978-1-78899-664-8

www.packtpub.com

`mapt.io`

Mapt is an online digital library that gives you full access to over 5,000 books and videos, as well as industry leading tools to help you plan your personal development and advance your career. For more information, please visit our website.

Why subscribe?

- Spend less time learning and more time coding with practical eBooks and Videos from over 4,000 industry professionals

- Improve your learning with Skill Plans built especially for you

- Get a free eBook or video every month

- Mapt is fully searchable

- Copy and paste, print, and bookmark content

PacktPub.com

Did you know that Packt offers eBook versions of every book published, with PDF and ePub files available? You can upgrade to the eBook version at `www.PacktPub.com` and as a print book customer, you are entitled to a discount on the eBook copy. Get in touch with us at `service@packtpub.com` for more details.

At `www.PacktPub.com`, you can also read a collection of free technical articles, sign up for a range of free newsletters, and receive exclusive discounts and offers on Packt books and eBooks.

Contributors

About the author

Igor Kucherenko is an Android developer at Techery, a software development company that uses Kotlin as the main language for Android development. Currently, he lives in Ukraine, where he is a speaker in the Kotlin Dnipro Community, which promotes Kotlin and shares knowledge with audiences at meetups. You can find his articles about Kotlin and Android development on Medium and a blog for Yalantis, where he worked previously.

I'd like to thank my colleague for sharing knowledge, and Packt Publishing for the opportunity to write this book; Russell Snyder for his help with many details; my wife for her patience while I was writing this book.

About the reviewer

Ganesh Samarthyam is a co-founder of CodeOps Technologies, a software technology, consultancy, and training company based in Bangalore. He has 16 years of experience in the IT industry, and his latest book, *Refactoring for Software Design Smells: Managing Technical Debt* by Morgan Kaufmann/Elsevier, has been translated to languages such as Korean and Chinese. Ganesh loves exploring anything and everything about technology in his free time.

Packt is searching for authors like you

If you're interested in becoming an author for Packt, please visit `authors.packtpub.com` and apply today. We have worked with thousands of developers and tech professionals, just like you, to help them share their insight with the global tech community. You can make a general application, apply for a specific hot topic that we are recruiting an author for, or submit your own idea.

Table of Contents

Preface

Kotlin is a statically typed programming language that is designed to interoperate with Java code. Since the kotlinc compiler generates the same bytecode as javac, migrating to a new code base doesn't require a lot of effort. Kotlin is a modern language that contains many features from different paradigms that allow you to write concise and safe code. In light of all these points, Kotlin is growing in popularity and increasing in the number of developers who use it.

The book starts by analyzing different performance metrics and debugging tools that help us to identify performance bottlenecks. It's important to understand how Kotlin and its modern features work under the hood; that's why we will inspect a lot of bytecode in the book. We will learn how to benchmark our code and avoid different types of resource leaks. The book ends with best practices that will help you to sum up all things that you've learned.

Who this book is for

This book is for developers who would like to gain deeper understanding of how Kotlin works under the hood. The material doesn't depend on a certain platform of framework, but it focuses on Java Virtual Machine. This book doesn't cover topics about Kotlin to JavaScript feature and Kotlin/Native. It's a good choice for client-side developers because it contains examples with user interfaces and multithreaded environments.

What this book covers

Chapter 1, *Identifying Performance Bottlenecks*, covers the reasons for performance issues and how they can impact the user experience and performance of the whole software product. It is an overview of the issues this book aims to resolve, and prepares the reader for the details of these issues in subsequent chapters.

Chapter 2, *Identifying Performance Issues*, presents performance as one of the leading challenges you will encounter while building any software application. Response speed is one of the critical criteria to analyze performance issues, and it closely correlates with the success of that software in the market. We can use different parameters to identify problems depending on the architecture and what technology is used in the implementation.

Chapter 3, *Learn How to Use Profiling Tools*, introduces various techniques of troubleshooting application code. We will look at the different profiling tools that measure space of memory, the frequency and duration of function calls, and which software is included in the IntelliJ IDEA platform for this purpose.

Chapter 4, *Functional Approach*, introduces the functional features of Kotlin. A significant one is the lambda expression, since it allows us to write functions in a much simpler way. We will figure out the bytecode of lambda and the equivalent code in Java to get an understanding of how to use it with minimal overhead.

Chapter 5, *Enhancing the Performance of Collections*, covers topics related to collections, including their innerworkings and performance enhancements. We will look at the Iterator pattern and its pros and cons.

Chapter 6, *Optimizing Access to Properties*, covers topics that relate to fields and properties. Virtual method calls are expensive, much more so than instance field lookups. In this chapter, readers will learn how to write the code in such a way as to avoid generation getters and setters in bytecode.

Chapter 7, *Preventing Unnecessary Overhead using Delegated Properties*, introduces a powerful mechanism that allows us to reduce the amount of code and separate the logic of an application. But we should remember that we have the same bytecode as Java under the hood, and it can be the reason for creating extra objects.

Chapter 8, *Ranges and Identifying Performance Issues*, introduces ranges in Kotlin that service to represent a sequence of values. This chapter covers some performance issues that can occur while you are working on this feature.

Chapter 9, *Multithreading and Reactive Programming*, covers basic coroutine-related topics, including concurrency and parallelism. It shows how to invoke long-term operations sequentially in order to avoid Callback hell.

Chapter 10, *Best Practices*, summarizes the book and contains general tips on how to avoid performance issues in an Android application. Readers will be given general rules that will help them avoid performance issues.

To get the most out of this book

To run examples from this book, you will need a computer running Windows, Linux, or Mac OS. You also need IntelliJ IDEA (Ultimate edition version is preferable) and Android Studio. You need basic knowledge of GitHub and Git to clone a project with examples.

Since Kotlin is an official language for Android development, Android Studio supports this language out of the box. For IntelliJ IDEA you need to install a plugin that is available for download from `https://plugins.jetbrains.com/plugin/6954-kotlin`.

Download the example code files

You can download the example code files for this book from your account at `www.packtpub.com`. If you purchased this book elsewhere, you can visit `www.packtpub.com/support` and register to have the files emailed directly to you.

You can download the code files by following these steps:

1. Log in or register at `www.packtpub.com`.
2. Select the **SUPPORT** tab.
3. Click on **Code Downloads & Errata**.
4. Enter the name of the book in the **Search** box and follow the onscreen instructions.

Once the file is downloaded, please make sure that you unzip or extract the folder using the latest version of:

- WinRAR/7-Zip for Windows
- Zipeg/iZip/UnRarX for Mac
- 7-Zip/PeaZip for Linux

The code bundle for the book is also hosted on GitHub at `https://github.com/PacktPublishing/Mastering-High-Performance-with-Kotlin`. In case there's an update to the code, it will be updated on the existing GitHub repository.

We also have other code bundles from our rich catalog of books and videos available at `https://github.com/PacktPublishing/`. Check them out!

Download the color images

We also provide a PDF file that has color images of the screenshots/diagrams used in this book. You can download it here: `https://www.packtpub.com/sites/default/files/downloads/MasteringHighPerformancewithKotlin_ColorImages.pdf`.

Conventions used

There are a number of text conventions used throughout this book.

`CodeInText`: Indicates code words in text, database table names, folder names, filenames, file extensions, pathnames, dummy URLs, user input, and Twitter handles. Here is an example: "To override `finalize()`, all you need to do is simply declare it without using the `override` keyword (and it can't be private)."

A block of code is set as follows:

```
class C {
    protected fun finalize() {
        // finalization logic
    }
}
```

Any command-line input or output is written as follows:

```
computation
CacheThread 8
NetworkThread 8
```

Bold: Indicates a new term, an important word, or words that you see onscreen. For example, words in menus or dialog boxes appear in the text like this. Here is an example: "The IntelliJ IDEA has a special function for this. Go to the `CalculatorMachine` class and open the **Generate** pane."

 Warnings or important notes appear like this.

 Tips and tricks appear like this.

Get in touch

Feedback from our readers is always welcome.

General feedback: Email `feedback@packtpub.com` and mention the book title in the subject of your message. If you have questions about any aspect of this book, please email us at `questions@packtpub.com`.

Errata: Although we have taken every care to ensure the accuracy of our content, mistakes do happen. If you have found a mistake in this book, we would be grateful if you would report this to us. Please visit `www.packtpub.com/submit-errata`, selecting your book, clicking on the Errata Submission Form link, and entering the details.

Piracy: If you come across any illegal copies of our works in any form on the Internet, we would be grateful if you would provide us with the location address or website name. Please contact us at `copyright@packtpub.com` with a link to the material.

If you are interested in becoming an author: If there is a topic that you have expertise in and you are interested in either writing or contributing to a book, please visit `authors.packtpub.com`.

Reviews

Please leave a review. Once you have read and used this book, why not leave a review on the site that you purchased it from? Potential readers can then see and use your unbiased opinion to make purchase decisions, we at Packt can understand what you think about our products, and our authors can see your feedback on their book. Thank you!

For more information about Packt, please visit `packtpub.com`.

1
Identifying Performance Bottlenecks

How well does it work? How fast is it? These questions mean essentially the same thing if we're talking about software. Although the question about saving technical resources isn't as relevant as it was in the early years of the computer industry, developers still should be careful about the efficiency of systems. Even though efficiency starts with hardware, modern computers have such large instruction sets that it's possible to use them in any manner.

Engineers spend a lot of time and effort to avoid a drain on the **Central Processing Unit** (**CPU**), to save battery life, or to make an animation of the user interface much smoother. So the question about performance is relevant nowadays, and software engineers should be careful with system resources.

Before we begin, let's review the topics we will be looking at:

- Reasons for performance issues
- Memory model
- Slow rendering

Reasons for performance issues

Performance is a complicated term that can include response time, the speed of data transmission, availability, and utilization of computer resources. First of all, we should remember that we develop software for users, and so we should concentrate on factors that affect their experience.

Different issues can influence overall system performance differently. In one case, we can have a slow rendering speed; in another case, the response time can be slow. Poor performance decreases productivity, damages the loyalty of customers, and costs the software industry millions of dollars annually. So it would be better to identify bottlenecks before they begin to have a negative influence on the user experience.

Today's customers have applications with legacy code that require upgrading throughputs and response time. Java is one of the most popular languages in the world. A lot of server-side mobile applications and software for SIM cards have been written in Java. But Java isn't a modern programming language. This is the main reason for the appearance of Kotlin. It allows you to write simpler and more reliable code. The fact that Kotlin can compile to the same bytecode as Java is why applications written in these different languages can have the same performance. That's why the question about migrating from Java to Kotlin is relevant nowadays, and developers should be prepared for it. We're going to uncover the main reasons for performance issues that relate to all applications that are based on the **Java Virtual Machine** (**JVM**) and consequently to Kotlin.

Memory management

Memory is one of the essential resources of a computer, and it's essential to manage it properly. Failure to do so can lead to slow performance and bugs such as arithmetic overflow, memory leaks, segmentation faults, and buffer overflows.

The primary purpose of a memory management system is to provide the ability to dynamically allocate the requested size of memory to programs and to release it for reuse when no longer needed. These systems perform management on two levels:

- Operating-system level
- Application level

We'll concentrate on the application level because it's the responsibility of an application software developer. The operating-system level is managed with an operating system.

There are two types of application-level management systems:

- Automatic memory management
- Manual memory management

Manual memory management assumes that the programmer uses manual instructions to release unused garbage. It's relevant to languages (still in wide use today) such as C and C++. The JVM has automatic memory management that involves the garbage collection.

Garbage collection

Garbage collection is a strategy for automatically detecting memory allocated to objects that are no longer usable in a program and returning that allocated memory to the pool of free memory locations. All memory management techniques, including garbage collection, take a significant proportion of a program's total processing time and, as a result, can greatly influence performance. With modern, optimized garbage collection algorithms, memory can be released faster than with manual memory management. But depending on the application, the opposite can also be true, and many developers prefer to deallocate memory themselves. One of the biggest advantages that manual memory management has is the ability to reclaim resources before an object is destroyed. This process is referred to as finalization, and we'll touch on it further because it can also be a performance issue.

Memory management is an essential process that's applied to the computer memory. Since the JVM uses automatic memory management with the garbage collection strategy we should know what it is and how it works.

Working principles of the garbage collector

The garbage collection strategy assumes that the developer doesn't explicitly release memory. Instead, the **garbage collector** (**GC**) finds objects that aren't being used anymore and destroys them. As GC sees it, there are two types of objects—reachable and unreachable. This principle is based on a set of root objects that are always reachable. An **object** is a root if it satisfies one of the following criteria:

- **Local variables**: They are stored in the stack of a thread. When a method, constructor, or initialization block is entered, local variables are created and become unreachable and available for the GC once they exit the scope of the method, constructor, or initialization block.
- **Active threads**: These are objects that hold other ones from the GC's point of view. So all these objects are a reference tree that will not be destroyed until the thread is terminated.
- **Static variables**: They are referenced by instances of the `Class` type where they're defined. The metadata of classes is kept in the Metaspace section of memory. This makes static variables de facto roots. When a `classLoader` loads and instantiates a new object of the `Class` type, static variables are created and can be destroyed during major garbage collection.

- **Java native interface references**: They are references to objects that are held in native code. These objects aren't available to the GC because they can be used outside the JVM environment. These references require manual management in native code. That's why they often become the reason for memory leaks and performance issues.

The following diagram illustrates a simplified schematic of references trees:

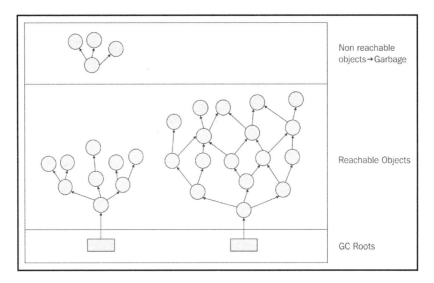

An object is reachable if it's a leaf from a reference tree that's reachable from the root object. If an object is unreachable, then it's available for the GC. Since the GC starts collecting at unpredictable times, it's hard to tell when the memory space will be deallocated.

To perform garbage collection, the JVM needs to stop the world. This means that the JVM stops all threads except those that are needed for garbage collection. This procedure guarantees that new objects aren't created and that old objects don't suddenly become unreachable while the GC is working. Modern GC implementations do as much work as possible in the background thread. For instance, the mark and sweep algorithm marks reachable objects while the application continues to run, and parallel collectors split a space of the heap into small sections, and a separate thread works on each one.

The memory space is divided into several primary generations—**young**, **old**, and **permanent**. The permanent generation contains static members and the metadata about classes and methods. Newly created objects belong to the young generation, and once there's no reference to any of them, it becomes available for minor garbage collection. After this, the surviving objects are moved to the old generation, and become available only for major garbage collection.

Impacts of garbage collection

Depends on algorithm, the performance of garbage collection can depend on the number of objects or the size of the heap. GC needs time to detect reachable and unreachable objects. During this step, automatic memory management might lose out to manual memory management because a developer may have already known which objects should be destroyed. And after this stop the world—also known as the **GC pause**—is invoked, the GC suspends execution of all threads to ensure the integrity of reference trees.

Heap fragmentation

When the JVM starts, it allocates heap memory from the operating system and then manages that memory. Whenever an application creates a new object, the JVM automatically allocates a block of memory with a size that's big enough to fit the new object on the heap. After sweeping, in most cases, memory becomes fragmented. Memory fragmentation leads to two problems:

- Allocation operations become more time consuming, because it's hard to find the next free block of sufficient size
- The unused space between blocks can become so great that the JVM won't be able to create a new object

The following diagram illustrates a fragmented memory heap:

To avoid these problems after each GC cycle, the JVM executes a compaction step. Compacting moves all reachable objects to one end of the heap and, in this way, closes all holes. The heap after compacting looks as follows:

These diagrams show how blocks are located before and after compacting. The drawback is that an application must also be suspended during this process.

Finalization

Finalization is a process of releasing resources. It's executed with a finalizer method that's invoked after an object becomes unreachable, but before its memory is deallocated. Finalization is a non-deterministic process because it's not known when garbage collection will occur, and it might never happen. This is in contrast to a destructor, which is a method called for finalization in languages with manual memory management.

The following diagram illustrates the simplified life cycle of an object:

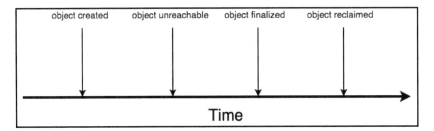

A destructor, in most languages, is the language-level term that means a method defined in a class by a programmer. A **finalizer** is an implementation-level term that means a method called by a system during object creation or destruction. Finalizers are needed to perform object-specific operations, cleaning or releasing resources that were used with an object. That's why they're most frequently instance methods.

Finalizers have several drawbacks:

- It may never be called promptly, so a software engineer cannot rely on it to do something important, such as persisting a state or releasing scarce resources.
- The invoking order of finalizers isn't specified.
- Garbage collection, and consequently the finalizer, runs when memory resources are terminated but not when it's time to release other scarce resources. So, it's not a good idea to use it to release limited resources.
- If too much work is performed in one finalizer, another one may start with a delay. And this may increase the total time of the garbage collection pause.
- A finalizer may cause synchronization issues as well because it can use shared variables.
- A finalizer in a superclass can also slow down garbage collection in a subclass because it can refer to the same fields.

To implement the finalizer in Java, a developer has to override the `finalize()` method of the `Object` class. The `Object` class has an empty implementation of the following method:

```
protected void finalize() throws Throwable { }
```

This method has good documentation with two interesting moments. The first is that the Java programming language doesn't guarantee which thread will invoke the `finalize()` method for any given object. It's guaranteed, however, that the thread that invokes the `finalize()` method will not be holding any user-visible synchronization locks when `finalize()` is invoked. If an uncaught exception is thrown by the `finalize()` method, the exception is ignored, and finalization of that object terminates. And the second interesting catch is that any exceptions that are thrown by the `finalize()` method cause the finalization of this object to be halted, but they are otherwise ignored.

A sample of overriding can be found, for instance, in the source code of the `FileInputStream` class:

```
@Override protected void finalize() throws IOException {
    try {
        if (guard != null) {
          guard.warnIfOpen();
        }
        close();
    } finally {
        try {
            super.finalize();
        } catch (Throwable t) {
            // for consistency with the RI, we must override
```

```
Object.finalize() to
            // remove the 'throws Throwable' clause.
            throw new AssertionError(t);
        }
    }
}
```

This implementation ensures that all resources for this stream are released when it's about to be garbage collected.

But in Kotlin, the root of the class hierarchy is `Any`, which does not have a `finalize()` method:

```
public open class Any {

    public open operator fun equals(other: Any?): Boolean

    public open fun hashCode(): Int

    public open fun toString(): String
}
```

But according to the Kotlin documentation: `https://kotlinlang.org/docs/reference/java-interop.html#finalize`, to override `finalize()`, all you need to do is simply declare it without using the `override` keyword (and it can't be private):

```
class C {
    protected fun finalize() {
        // finalization logic
    }
}
```

If you read to avoid finalizers and cleaners item of the effective Java book, you know that using finalizers to release resources is a common anti-pattern. To acquire resources in the constructor or initialization block and release it in the finalizer isn't a good approach. It's better to acquire the resources only when needed and release them once they're no longer needed. In other cases, using the `finalize()` method to release resources can cause resource and memory leaks.

Resource leaks

An operating system has several resources that are limited in number, for instance, files or internet sockets. A **resource leak** is a situation where a computer program doesn't release the resources it has acquired. The most common example is a case where files have been opened but haven't been closed:

```
fun readFirstLine() : String {
    val fileInputStream = FileInputStream("input.txt")
    val inputStreamReader = InputStreamReader(fileInputStream)
    val bufferedReader = BufferedReader(inputStreamReader)
    return bufferedReader.readLine()
}
```

In the preceding code snippet, the input.txt file hasn't been closed after being acquired and used. InputStream is an abstract superclass of all classes representing an input stream of bytes. It implements the Closeable single-method interface with a close() method. The subclasses of InputStream override this method to provide the ability to release the input stream, and in our case the file, correctly. So a correct version of the readFirstLine() method would look like this:

```
fun readFirstLine() : String? {
    var fileInputStream: FileInputStream? = null
    var inputStreamReader: InputStreamReader? = null
    var bufferedReader: BufferedReader? = null
    return try {
        fileInputStream = FileInputStream("input.txt")
        inputStreamReader = InputStreamReader(fileInputStream)
        bufferedReader = BufferedReader(inputStreamReader)
        bufferedReader.readLine()
    } catch (e: Exception) {
        null
    } finally {
        fileInputStream?.close()
        inputStreamReader?.close()
        bufferedReader?.close()
    }
}
```

 It's important to close a stream inside a finally section because if you do it at the end of the try section and an exception is thrown, then you'll have a file handle leak.

In this example, we can see how the dispose pattern is used with the `try-finally` special language construction. It's a design pattern for resource management that assumes use of the method usually called `close()`, `dispose()`, or `release()` to free the resources once they aren't needed. But since Kotlin 1.2, thanks to extension functions, we can write something like this:

```
fun readFirstLine(): String? = File("input.txt")
  .inputStream()
  .bufferedReader()
  .use { it.readLine() }
```

The `use` or `useLines` function executes the given block function on this resource and then closes it down correctly whether or not an exception is thrown.

> The `use` and `useLines` functions return the result of the block, which is very convenient, especially in our case.

The source code of the `use` function also uses the `try-finally` construction to ensure resources will be closed:

```
public inline fun <T : Closeable?, R> T.use(block: (T) -> R): R {
    var exception: Throwable? = null
    try {
        return block(this)
    } catch (e: Throwable) {
        exception = e
        throw e
    } finally {
        when {
            apiVersionIsAtLeast(1, 1, 0) -> this.closeFinally(exception)
            this == null -> {}
            exception == null -> close()
            else ->
              try {
                close()
              } catch (closeException: Throwable) {
                // cause.addSuppressed(closeException) // ignored here
              }
        }
    }
}
```

So scarce resources that have been acquired must be released. Otherwise, an application will suffer from a resource leak, for example, a file handle leak like the one we've just described. Another common reason for slow performance is a memory leak.

Memory leaks

A **memory leak** may happen when an object can't be collected and can't be accessed by running code. The situation when memory that is no longer needed isn't released is referred to as a memory leak. In an environment with a GC, such as the JVM, a memory leak may happen when a reference to an object that's no longer needed is still stored in another object. This happens due to logical errors in program code, when an object holds a reference to another one when the last isn't used and isn't accessible in the program code anymore. The following diagram represents this case:

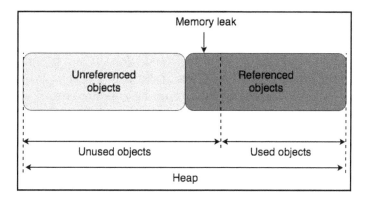

The GC cares about unreachable, also known as unreferenced, objects, but handling unused referenced objects depends on application logic. Leaked objects allocate memory, which means that less space is available for new objects. So if there's a memory leak, the GC will work frequently and the risk of the OutOfMemoryError exception increases.

Let's look at an example written in Kotlin of the popular RxJava2 library:

```
fun main(vars: Array<String>) {
    var memoryLeak: MemoryLeak? = MemoryLeak()
    memoryLeak?.start()
    memoryLeak = null
    memoryLeak = MemoryLeak()
    memoryLeak.start()
    Thread.currentThread().join()
}
```

```
class MemoryLeak {

    init {
        objectNumber ++
    }

    private val currentObjectNumber = objectNumber

    fun start() {
        Observable.interval(1, TimeUnit.SECONDS)
                .subscribe { println(currentObjectNumber) }
    }

    companion object {
        @JvmField
        var objectNumber = 0
    }
}
```

In this example, the `join()` method of the `main` thread is used to prevent the ending of application execution until other threads run. The `objectNumber` field of the `MemoryLeak` class counts created instances. Whenever a new instance of the `MemoryLeak` class is created, the value of `objectNumber` increments and is copied to the `currentObjectNumber` property.

The `MemoryLeak` class also has the `start()` method. This method contains an instance of `Observable` that emits an incremented number every second. `Observable` is the multi-valued base-reactive class that offers factory methods, intermediate operators, and the ability to consume synchronous and/or asynchronous reactive data-flows. `Observable` has many factory functions that create new instances to perform different actions. In our case, we'll use the `interval` function that takes two arguments—the sampling rate and the instance of the `TimeUnit` enum (https://docs.oracle.com/javase/7/docs/api/java/util/concurrent/TimeUnit.html), which is the time unit in which the sampling rate is defined. The `subscribe` method takes an instance of a class that has the `Consumer` type. The most common approach is to create a lambda to handle emitted values.

The `main` function is the starting point of our application. In this function, we create a new instance of the `MemoryLeak` class, then invoke the `start()` method. After this, we assign `null` to the `memoryLeak` reference and repeat the previous step.

This is the most common issue when using RxJava. The first instance of the `MemoryLeak` class cannot be collected because the passed `Consumer` obtains references to it. Hence one of the active threads, which is a `root` object, obtains references to the first instance of `MemoryLeak`. Since we don't have a reference to this object, it's unused, but it can't be collected. The output of the application looks as follows:

```
1
2
1
2
2
1
1
2
1
2
1
```

As you can see, both instances of `Observable` run and use the `currentObjectNumber` property, and both instances of the `MemoryLeak` class sequentially allocate memory. That's why we should release resources when an object is no longer needed. To deal with this issue, we have to rewrite the code as follows:

```
  fun main(vars: Array<String>) {
      var memoryLeak: NoMemoryLeak? = NoMemoryLeak()
      memoryLeak?.start()
+     memoryLeak?.disposable?.dispose()
      memoryLeak = NoMemoryLeak()
      memoryLeak.start()
      Thread.currentThread().join()
  }

  class NoMemoryLeak {

      init {
          objectNumber ++
      }

      private val currentObjectNumber = objectNumber

+     var disposable: Disposable? = null

      fun start() {
+         disposable = Observable.interval(1, TimeUnit.SECONDS)
                  .subscribe { println(currentObjectNumber) }
      }
```

```
        companion object {
            @JvmField
            var objectNumber = 0
        }
    }
```

And now the output looks like this:

```
2
2
2
2
2
2
```

The `subscribe()` method returns an instance of the `Disposable` type, which has the `dispose()` method. Using this approach, we can prevent the memory leak.

Using instances of mutable classes without overriding the `equals()` and `hashCode()` methods as keys for `Map` can also lead to a memory leak. Let's look at the following example:

```
class MutableKey(var name: String? = null)

fun main(vars: Array<String>) {
    val map = HashMap<MutableKey, Int>()
    map.put(MutableKey("someName"), 2)
    print(map[MutableKey("someName")])
}
```

The output will be the following:

```
null
```

The `get` method of `HashMap` uses the `hashCode()` and `equals()` methods of a key to find and return a value. The current implementation of the `MutableKey` class doesn't override these methods. That's why if you lose the reference to the original key instance, you won't be able to retrieve or remove the value. It's definitely a memory leak because `map` is a local variable and sequentially it's the `root` object.

We can remedy the situation by making the `MutableKey` class data. If a class is marked as `data`, the compiler automatically derives the `equals()` and `hashCode()` methods from all properties declared in the primary constructor. So the `MutableKey` class will look as follows:

```
data class MutableKey(var name: String? = null)
```

And now the output will be:

```
2
```

Now, this class works as expected. But we can face another issue with the `MutableKey` class. Let's rewrite `main` as follows:

```
fun main(vars: Array<String>) {
    val key = MutableKey("someName")

    val map = HashMap<MutableKey, Int>()
    map.put(key, 2)

    key.name = "anotherName"
    print(map[key])
}
```

Now, the output will be:

```
null
```

Because the hash, after re-assigning the `name` property, isn't the same as it was before:

```
fun main(vars: Array<String>) {
    val key = MutableKey("someName")

    println(key.hashCode())

    val map = HashMap<MutableKey, Int>()
    map.put(key, 2)

    key.name = "anotherName"

    println(key.hashCode())

    print(map[key])
}
```

The output will now be:

```
1504659871
-298337234
null
```

This means that our code isn't simple and reliable. And we can still have the memory leak. The concept of an immutable object is extremely helpful in this case. Using this concept, we can protect objects from corruption, which is exactly the issue we need to prevent.

A strategy of creating classes for immutable objects in Java is complex and includes the following key moments:

- Do not provide setters
- All fields have to be marked with the final and private modifiers
- Mark a class with the final modifier
- References that are held by fields of an immutable class should refer to immutable objects
- Objects that are composed by an immutable class have to also be immutable

An immutable class that is created according to this strategy may looks as follows:

```java
public final class ImmutableKey {


    private final String name;

    public ImmutableKey(String name) {
        this.name = name;

}
    public String getName() {
        return name;

}
  }
```

This is all very easy in Kotlin:

```kotlin
data class ImmutableKey(val name: String? = null)
```

All we need is it define all properties with `val` in `primary constructor`. We'll get a compiler error if we try to assign a new value to the `name` property. Immutability is an extremely powerful concept that allows us to implement some mechanisms, such as the String pool.

String pool

The **String pool** is a set of String objects stored in the *Permanent Generation* section of the heap. Under the hood, an instance of the String class is an array of chars. Each char allocates two bytes. The String class also has a cached hash that allocates four bytes, and each object has housekeeping information that allocates about eight bytes. And if we're talking about Java Development Kit 7 (http://grepcode.com/file/repository.grepcode. com/java/root/jdk/openjdk/7-b147/java/lang/String.java?av=f) or lower, the String class also has offset and length fields. Since String is the most used type, the instances of the String class allocate a significant part of the heap.

To reduce the load on memory, the JVM has the String pool as the implementation of the *Flyweight Design Pattern* because memory space can be crucial for low-memory devices such as mobile devices.

Whenever double quotes are used to create a new instance of the String class, the JVM first looks for an existing instance with the same value in the String pool. If an existing instance is found, a reference to it is returned. Otherwise, a new instance is created in the String pool and then the reference to it is returned. When we use a constructor, we force the creation of a new instance of the String class in the heap:

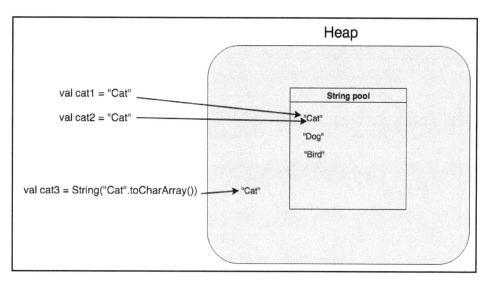

This technique is called **copy-on-write** (**COW**). The point is that when a copy of the object is requested, the reference to the existing object is returned instead of creating a new one. In code, it may look like this:

```
fun main(vars: Array<String>) {
    val cat1 = "Cat"
    val cat2 = "Cat"
    val cat3 = String("Cat".toCharArray())
    println(cat1 === cat2)
    println(cat1 === cat3)
}
```

The output:

```
true
false
```

Kotlin has its own `kotlin.String` class. It's not the same as the `java.lang.String` class. And `kotlin.String` doesn't have a constructor that takes another instance of the `String` class.

With the COW, when trying to modify an object through a particular reference, a real copy is created, the change is applied to it, and then the reference to the newly created object is returned. The following diagram illustrates this:

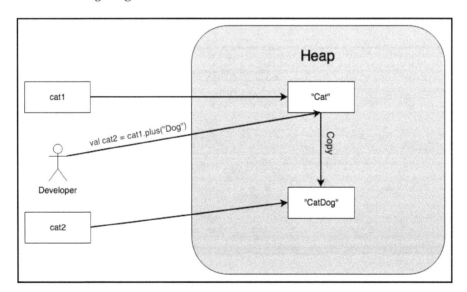

In code, it may look like this:

```
fun main(vars: Array<String>) {
    val cat1 = "Cat"
    val cat2 = cat1.plus("Dog")
    println(cat1)
    println(cat2)
    println(cat1 === cat2)
}
```

And here's the output:

```
Cat
CatDog
false
```

This technique is good for creating simple and reliable code and can be very useful in a concurrent application, as you can be sure that your object won't be corrupted with another thread.

Let's look at the following example:

```
class User(val id: Int = 0, val firstName: String = "", val lastName:
String = "")

fun main(vars: Array<String>) {
    val user = User()
    val building = "304a"

    val query = "SELECT id, firstName, lastName FROM Building " + building
+ " WHERE firstName = " + user.firstName
}
```

Each concatenation creates a new instance of String. So many unnecessary objects are created in this code. Instead of concatenation, we should use StringBuilder or **String Templates** (https://kotlinlang.org/docs/reference/basic-types.html#string-templates), which uses StringBuilder under the hood but is much simpler to use:

```
val query = "SELECT id, firstName, lastName FROM Building $building WHERE
firstName = ${user.firstName}"
```

But how can we put a `String` object into the String pool if we receive it from the outside? Here is how:

```
val firstLine: String
    get() = File("input.txt")
            .inputStream()
            .bufferedReader()
            .use { it.readLine() }

fun main(vars: Array<String>) {
    println(firstLine === firstLine)
}
```

This is the output:

false

To put the value of the `firstLine` variable in the String pool, we have to use the `intern()` method. When this method is invoked, if the pool already contains a string equal to the value of the object, then the reference to the `String` from the pool is returned. Otherwise, this object is added to the pool and a reference to this object is returned. The `intern()` method is an implementation of interning. It's a method for storing only one copy of each distinct value:

```
fun main(vars: Array<String>) {
    println(firstLine.intern() === firstLine.intern())
}
```

Here's the output:

true

You shouldn't abuse this method because the String pool is stored in the Permanent Generation section of the heap. And it can be collected only during major garbage collection.

Memory model

The memory model describes how the JVM interacts with a computer's memory. By computer memory, we mean not only **Random Access Memory** (**RAM**) but also registers and cache memory of the CPU. So we consider the memory model as a simplified abstraction of the hardware memory architecture.

We can consider the whole JVM as a model of a computer that provides the ability to run a program on a wide range of processors and operating systems.

An understanding of the Java Memory Model is important because it specifies how different threads interact in memory. Concurrent programming involves plenty of different pitfalls in synchronization between threads that have shared variables and compliance with the consistency of a sequence of operations.

The problem of concurrency and parallelism

While concurrency is executing independent subtasks out of order without affecting the final result, parallelism is the executing subtasks that are carried out simultaneously. Parallelism involves concurrency, but concurrency is not necessarily executed in a parallel manner.

The compiler feels free to reorder instructions to perform optimization. This means that there are cases in which accesses to variables, during the execution of a program, may differ from the order specified in the code. Data is moved between registers, caches, and RAM all the time. There are no requirements for the compiler to perform synchronization between threads perfectly because this would cost too much from the performance point of view. This leads to cases when different threads may read different values from the same shared variable. A simplified example of the case described here may look like this:

```
fun main(vars: Array<String>) {
    var sharedVariableA = 0
    var sharedVariableB = 0
    val threadPool = Executors.newFixedThreadPool(10)
    val threadA = Runnable {
        sharedVariableA = 3
        sharedVariableB = 4
    }
    val threadB = Runnable {
        val localA = sharedVariableA
        val localB = sharedVariableB
    }
    threadPool.submit(threadA)
    threadPool.submit(threadB)
}
```

In a body of the threadB thread, the value of the localA variable is 3, and the value of the localB variable is 4. But if the compiler reorders the operations, the final values of the local variables may differ. To get a better understanding of this issue, we need some knowledge of the internal system of the Java Memory Model.

Java Memory Model (JMM)

The JMM divides the memory space between thread stacks and the heap. Each application has at least one thread, which is referred to as the `main` thread. When a new thread starts, a new stack is created. If an application has several threads, the simplified memory model may look like this:

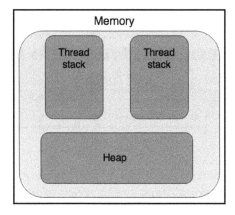

The thread stack is a stack of blocks. Whenever a thread calls a method, a new block is created and added to the stack. This is also referred to as the **call stack**. This block contains all the local variables that were created in its scope. The local variables cannot be shared between threads, even if threads are executing the same method. A block fully stores all local variables of primitive types and references to objects. One thread can only pass copies of local primitive variables or references to another thread:

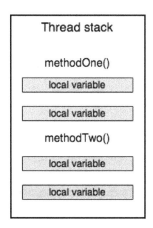

Kotlin doesn't have primitive types, in contrast to Java, but Kotlin does compile into the same bytecode as Java. And if you don't manipulate a variable in the same way as an object, then the generated bytecode will contain the variable of a primitive type:

```
fun main(vars: Array<String>) {

  val localVariable = 0
}
```

The simplified generated bytecode will look like this:

```
public final static main([Ljava/lang/String;)V

LOCALVARIABLE localVariable I L2 L3 1
```

But if you specify the type of the `localVariable` as `Nullable`, as follows:

```
val localVariable: Int? = null
```

Then this variable will be represented as an object in the bytecode:

```
LOCALVARIABLE localVariable Ljava/lang/Integer; L2 L3 1
```

All objects are contained in the heap even if they're local variables. In the case of local primitive variables, they'll be destroyed automatically when the execution point of a program leaves the scope of the method. The object can be destroyed only with the GC. So the use of local primitive variables is preferable. Since the Kotlin compiler applies optimizations to variables that can be primitive, in most cases the bytecode will contain variables of primitive types.

This diagram illustrates how two threads can share the same object:

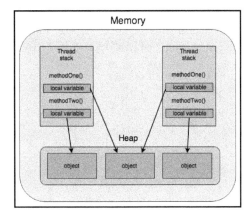

Synchronization

As we already know, the JMM is a simplified model of the hardware memory architecture. If a variable is used frequently, it can be copied to the CPU cache. If several threads have a shared variable, then several CPU caches have their own duplicate of this variable. This is needed to increase access speed to variables. The hardware memory architecture has a hierarchy that is illustrated in the following diagram:

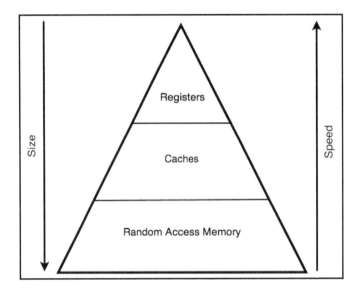

When several caches have duplicates of a variable that's stored in the main memory, the problem with visibility of shared objects may occur. This problem is referred to as a data race. This is a case when two or more threads change the values that were copied to caches. But one thread doesn't know about changes that were applied to the copied value by another thread. And when the thread updates the original variable in the main memory, the value that was assigned to the shared object by another thread can be erased.

The following example clarifies the described case. Two threads run on two CPUs at the same time. And they have a shared object with the count variable that's been copied to caches of both CPUs. Both threads increment the copied values at the same time. But these changes aren't visible to each other because the updates haven't been flushed back to the main memory yet. The following diagram illustrates this:

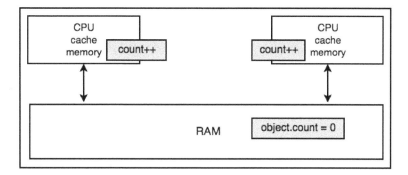

To solve the problem with synchronization, you can use the `volatile` keyword, synchronized methods, or blocks, and so on. But all of these approaches bring overhead and make your code complex. It's better just to avoid shared mutable objects and use only immutable objects in a multithreading environment. This strategy helps keep your code simple and reliable.

Slow rendering

Slow rendering is another performance issue that powerfully influences the user experience. Users expect interactive and smooth user interfaces, and that's where a development team needs to increasingly focus their efforts. It's not enough to make loading and the first rendering fast; the application also needs to perform well. Response time should be instantaneous, animations should be smooth, and scrolling should be stick-to-finger-fast. To create an application with an excellent experience, a developer needs to understand how to write code that runs as efficiently as possible.

Device refresh rate

Users interact and see the results of how an application reacts and updates the image on the display of the device, which is why it's an essential part that provides an excellent user experience. Manufacturers continue to improve display hardware, so it's important to understand some display characteristics.

The refresh rate of a display is how many times per second the image on the screen can be refreshed. It's measured in **hertz (Hz)**, so if the refresh rate of a display is 60 Hz, then the displayed picture cannot be updated more than 60 times per second.

The refresh rate that leads to a good experience depends on the purpose. Movies in movie theaters run at just 24 Hz, while the old TV standards were 50 Hz and 60 Hz. A typical monitor for a personal computer has a 60 Hz refresh rate, but the latest gaming displays can reach 240 Hz.

Since the device refresh rate is a hardware characteristic and a software developer can't influence it, the frame rate is of more interest. The following (from `https://developer.apple.com/library/content/documentation/DeviceInformation/Reference/iOSDeviceCompatibility/Displays/Displays.html`) shows the refresh rates and recommended frame rates for popular devices:

Device	Refresh rate	Recommended frame rates
iPhone X	60 Hz	60, 30, 20
iPhone 8 Plus	60 Hz	60, 30, 20
iPhone 8	60 Hz	60, 30, 20
iPhone 7 Plus	60 Hz	60, 30, 20
iPhone 7	60 Hz	60, 30, 20
iPhone 6s Plus	60 Hz	60, 30, 20
iPhone 6s	60 Hz	60, 30, 20
iPhone SE	60 Hz	60, 30, 20
iPhone 6 Plus	60 Hz	60, 30, 20
iPhone 6	60 Hz	60, 30, 20
iPad Pro 12.9-inch (2nd generation)	120 Hz maximum	120, 60, 40, 30, 24, 20
iPad Pro 10.5-inch	120 Hz maximum	120, 60, 40, 30, 24, 20
iPad Pro (12.9-inch)	60 Hz	60, 30, 20
iPad Pro (9.7-inch)	60 Hz	60, 30, 20
iPad Mini 4	60 Hz	60, 30, 20

Frame rate

The human brain receives and processes visual information continuously. This can be used to create the illusion of motion when images follow each other fast enough. When an animation or transition runs or the user scrolls the page, the application needs to put up a new picture for each screen refresh. How many images software shows per second is the **frame rate**, and it's measured in **frames per second** (**FPS**):

- A rate of 10 to 12 frames per second is referred to as clearly motion, and, in this case, a user retains awareness of individual pages.
- A 24 frames per second rate with motion-blurring technology is enough to see fluid movement and is enough for the film industry.
- A 30 frame per second rate is sufficient for movies, but without special effects.
- 60 or more frames per second is what most people see as high-quality, smooth motion:

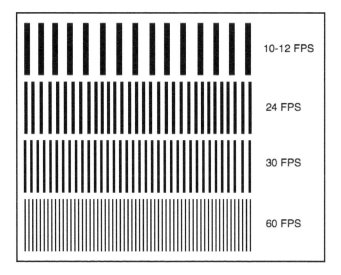

The act of generating a frame from an application and displaying it is referred to as **user interface rendering**. According to the table with recommended frame rates for popular devices, to be sure that a user interacts with an application smoothly, the application should render one frame each 16.6 ms to display 60 frames per second. The developer has to take into account that the system also requires some time to draw a frame, so it's not a good idea to plan to own all of that 16 ms, and it would be better to count on 10 ms. When an application fails to meet this budget, the frame rate drops and the content stutters on the screen.

It's essential to understand how to get smooth motion with a high frame rate. The human eye is extremely sensitive to motion inconsistencies. An application can display on average 60 frames per second, but it's enough to have only one frame that takes more than 16 ms to render, for the user to see something that we call **hitching**, **lag**, or **jank**. If the device's refresh rate is higher than the frame rate, the monitor displays repeated renderings of identical frames. This diagram illustrates a simplified view of jank:

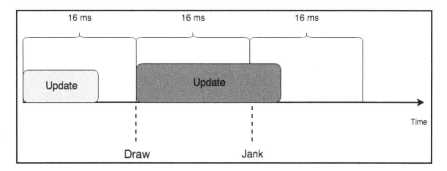

Summary

In this chapter, we presented the most common reasons for performance issues. We'll talk about them in more depth in the next chapters. We compared several examples in Java and Kotlin to know how to use features of these languages to prevent performance bottlenecks. We also introduced the most common things that influence the user experience of the whole application.

In the next chapter, we'll introduce different tools and practices for identifying performance issues.

2
Identifying Indicators of Performance Issues

So far, you have an understanding of what performance is. You also know which system bottlenecks lead to performance issues and how they do so. Now, we're ready to talk about how to identify these problems.

Different implementations of the same functionality can impact the performance of the whole application in different ways. It's hard to make the right choice between several approaches if you're guided by your assumptions. Therefore, we should measure performance but not make our choice based on a guess.

Measurement is a significant part of everyday management and technical activities. It's important because measurement gives us the numbers—the objective information—that we need to make informed decisions that improve performance. From the developer's point of view, performance measurement is the process of collecting, analyzing, and reporting information about the performance of an application. This is a vast topic, but a software engineer should know how to detect and recognize performance issues during the testing and post-release stages. That's why we'll touch on the topics most related to developers.

In this chapter, we'll cover the following topics:

- Benchmarking
- General performance metrics

Benchmarking

It's difficult to compare the performance of algorithms simply by looking at their descriptions or pseudocode. It's better to run actual implementations on a real system. This method of measurement is called **benchmarking**. There are three categories of benchmark:

- **Microbenchmarks**: These are metrics showing the performance of certain functions. They assume that a small piece of business logic is contained in a single function, and we simply measure how fast this function runs.
- **Macrobenchmarks**: These are the opposite of microbenchmarks; they test the entire application.
- **Mesobenchmarks**: These are something in-between, measuring features or workflows.

Large applications more or less contain certain critical pieces of code. The JVM is an adaptive virtual machine, meaning it optimizes running code in many ways. Obtaining metrics that are meaningful is actually difficult, which is why microbenchmarks are the most interesting for developers.

Microbenchmarks

Microbenchmarking is used if we want to know which methods perform better than others. A naive approach would wrap the called function inside a block of a `measureTimeMillis` or `measureNanoTime` function. These functions just calculate the difference between `start` and `stop` timestamps:

```
public inline fun measureTimeMillis(block: () -> Unit) : Long {
    val start = System.currentTimeMillis()
    block()
    return System.currentTimeMillis() - start
}
```

At a first glance, this approach gives us an idea about the performance of the code inside the `block`, but if we perform several experiments, it will be clear that this is the wrong approach. We've already touched on how the JVM executes and changes programming code to perform optimizations. When lines of code are executed, the JVM collects information about them. It will then try to optimize them and collect new information the next time it executes these same lines. Therefore, we have to take into account this factor and measure code after a warm-up to simulate real-world conditions.

To implement microbenchmarking correctly, you have to use the Java Microbenchmark Harness.

Java Microbenchmark Harness (JMH)

The JMH is an open source project that helps you to implement microbenchmarking correctly. You can be sure that this toolkit is one of the best because it's developed by the same people who work on the JVM.

The recommended way to work with JMH is by using Maven. You can install Maven using the instructions at the following link: http://maven.apache.org/install.html. Then, you can execute the following command to generate a test project:

```
mvn archetype:generate \
        -DinteractiveMode=false \
        -DarchetypeGroupId=org.openjdk.jmh \
        -DarchetypeArtifactId=jmh-java-benchmark-archetype \
        -DgroupId=org.sample \
        -DartifactId=test \
        -Dversion=1.0
```

The generated project will have the following structure:

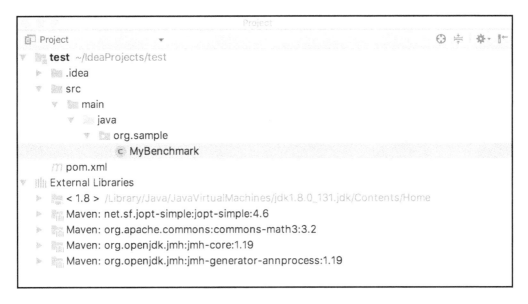

And the `MyBenchmark` file will look like this:

```
public class MyBenchmark {

    @Benchmark
    public void testMethod() {
        // This is a demo/sample template for building your JMH benchmarks.
Edit as needed.
        // Put your benchmark code here.
    }


}
```

If you want to generate a project with another name and package, you have to specify arguments using the -DgroupId and -DartifactId parameters. Now, you can write your own implementation of testMethod(), for instance:

```
@Benchmark
public void testMethod() {
    int a = 3;
    int b = 4;
    int c = a + b;
}
```

Run the mvn clean install command in the root folder of the project and the target folder will be generated. At this point, the structure of your project will look as follows:

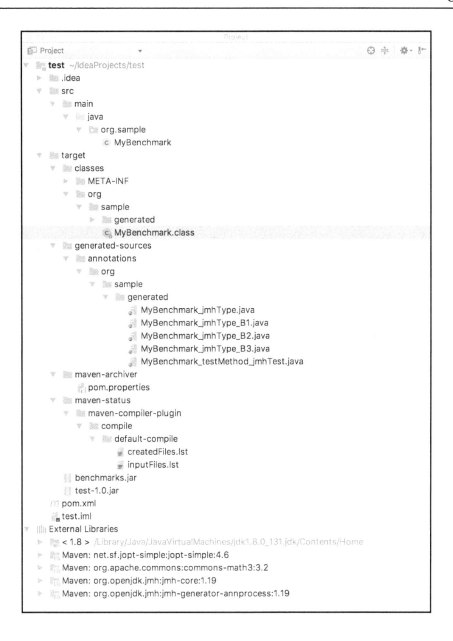

The most important file for our present purposes is `benchmarks.jar`. It contains the compiled `MyBenchmark` class and all JMH classes needed to run the `.jar` file. If you're going to add any external dependencies, you have to declare them inside the `pom.xml` file. Now you have a platform-independent `.jar` file, so you can run your test on any machine that has the JVM installed. Here's the command for running the test:

```
java -jar target/benchmarks.jar
```

In the output, you can see that the default configuration is `10` forks by `20` warm-ups, with simple iterations:

```
# Run progress: 90.00% complete, ETA 00:00:40
# Fork: 10 of 10
# Warmup Iteration 1: 2268891595.825 ops/s
# Warmup Iteration 2: 2028918125.250 ops/s
# Warmup Iteration 3: 2410600803.077 ops/s
......
# Warmup Iteration 17: 2224632990.097 ops/s
# Warmup Iteration 18: 2190560330.537 ops/s
# Warmup Iteration 19: 2117820907.659 ops/s
# Warmup Iteration 20: 2364498478.602 ops/s
Iteration 1: 2851568284.147 ops/s
Iteration 2: 2539539878.294 ops/s
Iteration 3: 2332746312.271 ops/s
.....
Iteration 17: 2389690978.812 ops/s
Iteration 18: 2285020290.690 ops/s
Iteration 19: 2220938195.822 ops/s
Iteration 20: 2242128929.564 ops/s
```

And the result looks like this:

```
Result "org.sample.MyBenchmark.testMethod":
2273140780.281 ±(99.9%) 60161283.208 ops/s [Average]
(min, avg, max) = (1065162420.546, 2273140780.281, 2989552931.957), stdev =
254726640.198
CI (99.9%): [2212979497.074, 2333302063.489] (assumes normal distribution)
# Run complete. Total time: 00:06:49
Benchmark              Mode  Cnt Score Error Units
MyBenchmark.testMethod thrpt 200 2273140780.281 ± 60161283.208 ops/s
```

The `ops/s` measure is the number of operations per second, or how many times the JMH can execute your method in one second. This number points to the fact that the default mode is `Throughput`. You can change this using the `OptionsBuilder` class:

```
public static void main(String[] args) throws RunnerException {
    Options opt = new OptionsBuilder()
            .include(MyBenchmark.class.getSimpleName())
            .forks(1)
            .measurementIterations(1)
            .mode(Mode.AverageTime)
            .build();

    new Runner(opt).run();
}
```

Or by using the special annotation `@BenchmarkMode` for methods. You can also use command-line arguments to set up the number of iterations and forks; for instance:

```
java -jar target/benchmarks.jar MyBenchmark -wi 5 -i 5 -f 1
```

In this case, we requested five warm-up and measurement iterations and a single fork.

Benchmark modes

You can find examples of how to use the JMH at the following link: `http://hg.openjdk.java.net/code-tools/jmh/file/tip/jmh-samples/src/main/java/org/openjdk/jmh/samples/`. One way is by using the `JMHSample_02_BenchmarkModes` class, which demonstrates the use of different modes. There are five modes:

- `Mode.Throughput`: This means that the benchmark method is being continuously invoked in a time-bound iteration and calculates how many times this method can be invoked.
- `Mode.AverageTime`: This measures similarly to `Mode.Throughput`, but calculates the average execution time.
- `Mode.SampleTime`: This measures similarly to `Mode.Throughput`, but samples the execution time for time-bound iterations.

- `Mode.SingleShotTime`: This measures the invocation time of a single method, which can be useful for cold startup testing. Using this mode, you specify that you don't want to call the benchmark method continuously.
- `Mode.All`: This does all of the above. Multiple modes let you specify modes that you want separated by commas—`@BenchmarkMode({Mode.Throughput, Mode.AverageTime, Mode.SampleTime, Mode.SingleShotTime})`.

We could rewrite our `testMethod()` as follows:

```
@Benchmark
@BenchmarkMode(Mode.AverageTime)
public void testMethod() {
    int a = 3;
    int b = 4;
    int c = a + b;
}
```

And by running it with five iterations and a single fork, the output will be as follows:

```
# Run progress: 0.00% complete, ETA 00:00:10
# Fork: 1 of 1
# Warmup Iteration 1: ≈ 10⁻⁹ s/op
# Warmup Iteration 2: ≈ 10⁻⁹ s/op
# Warmup Iteration 3: ≈ 10⁻⁹ s/op
# Warmup Iteration 4: ≈ 10⁻⁹ s/op
# Warmup Iteration 5: ≈ 10⁻⁹ s/op
Iteration 1: ≈ 10⁻⁹ s/op
Iteration 2: ≈ 10⁻⁹ s/op
Iteration 3: ≈ 10⁻⁹ s/op
Iteration 4: ≈ 10⁻⁹ s/op
Iteration 5: ≈ 10⁻⁹ s/op

Result "org.sample.MyBenchmark.testMethod":
≈ 10⁻⁹ s/op

# Run complete. Total time: 00:00:10

Benchmark              Mode Cnt Score Error Units
MyBenchmark.testMethod avgt 5 ≈ 10⁻⁹ s/op
```

This means that the average execution time for `testMethod()` is 10^{-9} which is equal to 0.000000001 seconds. If you want to get the results in another time unit, you have to use the `@OutputTimeUnit` annotation.

Benchmark time units

If we want to get the result in a more readable format, we can specify a time unit. In our case, it would be better to use NANOSECONDS. To do so, we can rewrite our method as follows:

```
@Benchmark
@BenchmarkMode(Mode.AverageTime)
@OutputTimeUnit(TimeUnit.NANOSECONDS)
public void testMethod() {
    int a = 3;
    int b = 4;
    int c = a + b;
}
```

The output will now be:

```
# Run progress: 0.00% complete, ETA 00:00:10
# Fork: 1 of 1
# Warmup Iteration 1: 0.345 ns/op
# Warmup Iteration 2: 0.342 ns/op
# Warmup Iteration 3: 0.342 ns/op
# Warmup Iteration 4: 0.337 ns/op
# Warmup Iteration 5: 0.342 ns/op
Iteration 1: 0.336 ns/op
Iteration 2: 0.333 ns/op
Iteration 3: 0.342 ns/op
Iteration 4: 0.340 ns/op
Iteration 5: 0.340 ns/op

Result "org.sample.MyBenchmark.testMethod":
0.338 ±(99.9%) 0.015 ns/op [Average]
(min, avg, max) = (0.333, 0.338, 0.342), stdev = 0.004
CI (99.9%): [0.323, 0.353] (assumes normal distribution)
# Run complete. Total time: 00:00:10

Benchmark               Mode Cnt Score Error Units
MyBenchmark.testMethod avgt 5    0.338 ± 0.015 ns/op
```

A 0.338 ns/op result is much easier to interpret than 10^{-9} s/op. You can specify any TimeUnit:

- NANOSECONDS
- MICROSECONDS
- MILLISECONDS
- SECONDS

- MINUTES
- HOURS
- DAYS

Let's suppose that our variables, a and b, require some time for initialization or are members of some global state. How can we share them between several benchmark methods? How can we initialize them before a scope of a benchmark method? For this, we can use a benchmark state.

Benchmark state

Our `testMethod()` function is a simple example, but most of the time our method with a critical piece of code depends on a state. **State** is a set of variables on which our code depends, but we don't want to initialize them in a benchmark method, and we need to maintain this state while the benchmark is running. Since the JMH is heavily used to build benchmarks with concurrent code, the concept of state-bearing objects was implemented. To implement the state class, you need to follow these rules:

- The class must be declared as public
- You can't use inner classes, but you can use nested classes that are declared with the static modifier
- The class must have a public constructor without arguments

A state class contains state variables, and if you specify an instance of this class as an argument it will be provided as a parameter to the `@Benchmark` method. In code, it might look as follows:

```
import org.openjdk.jmh.annotations.*;
import java.util.concurrent.TimeUnit;

public class MyBenchmark {

    @State(Scope.Thread)
    public static class MyState {
        int a = 3;
        int b = 4;
    }

    @Benchmark
    @BenchmarkMode(Mode.AverageTime)
    @OutputTimeUnit(TimeUnit.NANOSECONDS)
```

```
public void testMethod(MyState myState) {
    int c = myState.a + myState.b;
}

}
```

We use a state in this example because the `testMethod` uses two constant values and the compiler can optimize this moment and just use the final result instead of calculations. If you look at the output, you'll see that the result time has doubled:

```
Result "org.sample.MyBenchmark.testMethod":
0.671 ±(99.9%) 0.071 ns/op [Average]
(min, avg, max) = (0.656, 0.671, 0.702), stdev = 0.018
CI (99.9%): [0.600, 0.743] (assumes normal distribution)
# Run complete. Total time: 00:00:10
Benchmark                Mode Cnt Score Error Units
MyBenchmark.testMethod avgt 5    0.671 ± 0.071 ns/op
```

The `@State` annotation takes an instance of the `Scope` enum, which defines how to share the instance of the `MyState` class between threads.

State scope

The JMH provides three scopes, allowing you to reuse a state object across multiple invocations of benchmark methods:

- **Thread**: Each thread has its own copy of the state
- **Group**: Each group of threads has its own copy of the state
- **Benchmark**: All threads share the same state instance

Fixture methods

Since a state object can be kept during the whole lifetime of the benchmark, it would useful to have methods that do state housekeeping. This concept is implemented with the usual fixture methods that you might encounter in JUnit or TestNG. You can only write these methods inside a class that's declared with the `@State` annotation, and these methods can only be invoked by threads which are using the state. In this way, the thread-local context is created and you don't have to use thread synchronization.

The method for initializing must be marked with the @Setup annotation and the method that's declared with the @TearDown annotation will be invoked at the end of the object's lifetime. The following code example demonstrates how this concept works:

```
@State(Scope.Thread)
public class MyBenchmark {

    double x;

    @Setup
    public void prepare() {
        System.out.println("prepare");
        x = Math.PI;
    }

    @TearDown
    public void check() {
        System.out.println("check");
        assert x > Math.PI : "Nothing changed?";
    }

    @Benchmark
    public void measureRight() {
        x++;
    }

    @Benchmark
    public void measureWrong() {
        double x = 0;
        x++;
    }
}
```

The output will contain prepare and check messages, which talk about the start and the end of each scope. The measureRight() method obviously does the correct thing. Incrementing the x field in the state.check() benchmark will never fail this way because we're always guaranteed to have at least one benchmark call. However, the measureWrong() method will fail the check() method, because we deliberately have the typo, and it will only increment the local variable. This shouldn't pass the check, and the JMH will fail to run.

Levels of fixture methods

To control when fixture methods should be run, you can use at least three available options:

- **Trial**: Specifies that a method should be invoked before or after the entire benchmark run
- **Iteration**: Specifies that a method should be invoked before or after the benchmark iteration
- **Invocation**: Specifies that a method should be invoked before or after the benchmark method invocation

You can pass one of these objects as a parameter to the `@Setup` or `@TearDown` annotations.

Writing good benchmarks

The JMH can't handle all cases related to warming up and optimizing the JVM. There are cases when you just can't rely on the JMH. The most common pitfall is that the JVM may optimize your code when it's executed inside the benchmark, but inside a real application these optimizations may be not applied. Another of these pitfalls relates to loops.

The pitfalls of loops

There are a lot of optimizations related to loops. Let's investigate one more JMH example (`http://hg.openjdk.java.net/code-tools/jmh/file/ef50cc696984/jmh-samples/src/main/java/org/openjdk/jmh/samples/JMHSample_11_Loops.java`), which measures how much time it takes to sum two integers:

```
@State(Scope.Thread)
@BenchmarkMode(Mode.AverageTime)
@OutputTimeUnit(TimeUnit.NANOSECONDS)
public class MyBenchmark {

    int x = 1;
    int y = 2;
    @Benchmark
    public int measureRight() {
        return (x + y);
    }
    private int reps(int reps) {
        int s = 0;
        for (int i = 0; i < reps; i++) {
            s += (x + y);
        }
```

```
            return s;
    }
    @Benchmark
    @OperationsPerInvocation(1)
    public int measureWrong_1() {
        return reps(1);
    }

    @Benchmark
    @OperationsPerInvocation(10)
    public int measureWrong_10() {
        return reps(10);
    }

    @Benchmark
    @OperationsPerInvocation(100)
    public int measureWrong_100() {
        return reps(100);
    }

    @Benchmark
    @OperationsPerInvocation(1000)
    public int measureWrong_1000() {
        return reps(1000);
    }

    @Benchmark
    @OperationsPerInvocation(10000)
    public int measureWrong_10000() {
        return reps(10000);
    }

    @Benchmark
    @OperationsPerInvocation(100000)
    public int measureWrong_100000() {
        return reps(100000);
    }

}
```

The `measureRight()` method represents a case of correct measurement using the JMH. The `reps` method is an example of a simplified naive use of the JMH to measure a loop. The `measureWrong_*` methods represent wrong measurements with different repetition counts. The `@OperationsPerInvocation` annotation is used to get the individual operation cost.

In the output, you may notice that the larger the repetition count, the lower the measured cost of the operation:

```
Benchmark                           Mode Cnt  Score Error Units
MyBenchmark.measureRight            avgt 5    3.531 ± 6.938 ns/op
MyBenchmark.measureWrong_1          avgt 5    2.695 ± 0.365 ns/op
MyBenchmark.measureWrong_10         avgt 5    0.297 ± 0.047 ns/op
MyBenchmark.measureWrong_100        avgt 5    0.033 ± 0.002 ns/op
MyBenchmark.measureWrong_1000       avgt 5    0.030 ± 0.002 ns/op
MyBenchmark.measureWrong_10000      avgt 5    0.025 ± 0.003 ns/op
MyBenchmark.measureWrong_100000     avgt 5    0.022 ± 0.002 ns/op
```

This happens because the loop is heavily pipelined, and the operation to be measured is hosted from the loop. This means that the compiler optimizes the code and calculates the final result without a loop.

Dead Code Elimination

Another downfall of benchmarks is **Dead Code Elimination** (DCE). The JVM reduces computations that are redundant or eliminates them completely. Let's come back to our first implementation of the `testMethod()` method:

```
@Benchmark
public void testMethod() {
    int a = 3;
    int b = 4;
    int c = a + b;
}
```

In this example, the last line will be eliminated, but it's a significant part of our benchmark. The JMH provides the essential infrastructure to fight this issue. We can just return the result of computation as follows:

```
@Benchmark
public int testMethod() {
    int a = 3;
    int b = 4;
    return a + b;
}
```

The returned result is implicitly consumed by black holes.

Using black holes

You can use an instance of `Blackhole` explicitly, but it's really useful if you're going to consume several values with the black hole. In another case, this approach just affects readability and it would be better to just return the value. The next example demonstrates correct and incorrect cases:

```
@BenchmarkMode(Mode.AverageTime)
@OutputTimeUnit(TimeUnit.NANOSECONDS)
@State(Scope.Thread)
public class MyBenchmark {

    double x1 = Math.PI;
    double x2 = Math.PI * 2;

    @Benchmark
    public double baseline() {
        return Math.log(x1);
    }

    @Benchmark
    public double measureWrong() {
        Math.log(x1);
        return Math.log(x2);
    }

    @Benchmark
    public double measureRight_1() {
        return Math.log(x1) + Math.log(x2);
    }

    @Benchmark
    public void measureRight_2(Blackhole bh) {
        bh.consume(Math.log(x1));
        bh.consume(Math.log(x2));
    }

}
```

The output shows how the JVM eliminates the first line of the `measureWrong()` method:

```
Benchmark                           Mode  Cnt  Score Error  Units
MyBenchmark.baseline                avgt   5   24.385 ± 1.559 ns/op
MyBenchmark.measureRight_1          avgt   5   43.861 ± 4.813 ns/op
MyBenchmark.measureRight_2          avgt   5   47.041 ± 4.800 ns/op
MyBenchmark.measureWrong            avgt   5   24.447 ± 2.333 ns/op
```

Constant folding

Constant folding is the flip side of the DCE. If your calculation is based on constants and the result is often exactly the same, the JVM will detect this and replace the calculation with the result. To make sure this doesn't happen, we can move the computation outside the internal JMH loop. Constant folding can be prevented by always reading the inputs from non-final instance fields of a state object. In this case, the result will be based on fields of the state object:

```
@Benchmark
public int testMethod() {
    int a = 3;
    int b = 4;
    return a + b;
}
```

So, in the preceding code, the JVM can detect that the result value is based on two constants, a and b, and can replace our code with this:

```
public class MyBenchmark {
    @Benchmark
    public int testMethod() {
        int c = 3;
        return c;
    }
}
```

Or it can just return 3 or replace the invocation of this method with 3. To solve this problem, you should rewrite the code as follows:

```
public class MyBenchmark {

    @State(Scope.Thread)
    public static class MyState {
        int a = 3;
        int b = 4;
    }
```

```
@Benchmark
@BenchmarkMode(Mode.AverageTime)
@OutputTimeUnit(TimeUnit.NANOSECONDS)
public int testMethod(MyState state) {
    return state.a + state.b;
}

}
```

Kotlin benchmarks

The JetBrains team has prepared a repository on GitHub (`https://github.com/JetBrains/kotlin-benchmarks`) with many examples of how to use the JMH with Kotlin. This repository contains identical examples written in Java:

The repository also contains identical examples in Kotlin:

This lets us compare how fast functions written in Kotlin and Java run. If you run these benchmarks, the output will be as follows:

```
AbstractMethodBenchmark.sortStrings                           10       avgt 523.000              ns/op
AbstractMethodBenchmark.sortStrings                           1000     avgt 46534.937            ns/op
AbstractMethodBenchmark.sortStrings                           100000   avgt 5610020.939          ns/op
AbstractMethodBenchmark.sortStringsWithComparator             10       avgt 2256.651             ns/op
AbstractMethodBenchmark.sortStringsWithComparator             1000     avgt 1239050.026          ns/op
AbstractMethodBenchmark.sortStringsWithComparator             100000   avgt 107923516.400        ns/op
AbstractMethodBenchmark.sortStringsWithComparatorLambda       10       avgt 2677.882             ns/op
AbstractMethodBenchmark.sortStringsWithComparatorLambda       1000     avgt 1191127.699.         ns/op
AbstractMethodBenchmark.sortStringsWithComparatorLambda       100000   avgt 121202897.778        ns/op
AbstractMethodBenchmark.sortStringsWithComparatorSAM          10       avgt 2277.184             ns/op
AbstractMethodBenchmark.sortStringsWithComparatorSAM          1000     avgt 1376984.133          ns/op
AbstractMethodBenchmark.sortStringsWithComparatorSAM          100000   avgt 102603110.300        ns/op
AbstractMethodBenchmarkJava.sortStrings                       10       avgt 294.954              ns/op
AbstractMethodBenchmarkJava.sortStrings                       1000     avgt 51724.762            ns/op
AbstractMethodBenchmarkJava.sortStrings                       100000   avgt 4917147.471          ns/op
AbstractMethodBenchmarkJava.sortStringsWithComparator         10       avgt 1815.581             ns/op
AbstractMethodBenchmarkJava.sortStringsWithComparator         1000     avgt 931273.516           ns/op
AbstractMethodBenchmarkJava.sortStringsWithComparator         100000   avgt 89377734.417         ns/op
```

IDEA JMH plugin

You can download and install the JMH plugin for Intellij IDEA for more convenient use. You can find the source code for this plugin on GitHub at the following link: `https://github.com/artyushov/idea-jmh-plugin`.

This plugin has the following features:

- Generating `@Benchmark` method
- Running a separate `@Benchmark` method
- Running all `@Benchmark` methods in a class

General performance metrics

Benchmarking is a small part of performance testing. The main focus of performance testing is checking software:

- **Speed**: To determine how fast the application responds
- **Scalability**: To determine the maximum number of users that an application can handle
- **Stability**: To determine how the application invokes its functions under different loads

Types of performance testing

The most common performance problems revolve around **response time**, **speed**, **load time**, and **scalability**. These issues impact the most important attribute of an application: speed. Therefore, the main purpose of performance testing is to make sure that your application runs fast enough to keep a user's attention. There are a lot of different types of performance testing, for instance:

- Benchmark testing (we're already familiar with this)
- Load testing, which determines how an application works under anticipated user loads
- Volume testing, which tests what happens when a large amount of data populates a database
- Scalability testing, which determines how an application invokes functions with a large number of users
- Stress testing, which involves testing an application under extreme workloads

Performance testing process

Performance testing can be adapted for different purposes such as meeting pre-defined criteria or comparing the performance of two different systems. The following diagram shows the general stages of the performance testing process:

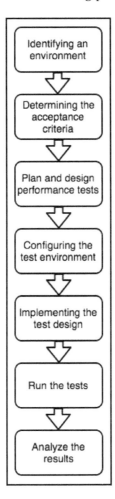

Now, let's discuss the various stages in performance testing:

- **Identifying the environment**: Getting an understanding of the hardware, software, and network configuration
- **Determining acceptance criteria**: Establishing goals and constraints for throughput, response times, and resource allocation
- **Planning and designing performance tests**: Identifying key scenarios to test for all possible use cases
- **Configuring the test environment**: Preparing to execute the testing
- **Implementing test design**: Creating the performance tests
- **Running the tests**: Executing and monitoring the tests
- **Analyzing results**: Consolidating, analyzing, and sharing test results

Overview of performance testing tools

There are a wide variety of performance testing tools. Your choice of tool depends on many factors, which includs platform and hardware requirements. But at any rate, you need these tools because they make testing much easier.

JMeter

JMeter is open source software that's designed to establish and test functional behavior and measure performance. You can use JMeter to analyze and measure the performance of web applications.

The following diagram from the introductory page (`https://www.guru99.com/introduction-to-jmeter.html`) represents the completed JMeter workflow:

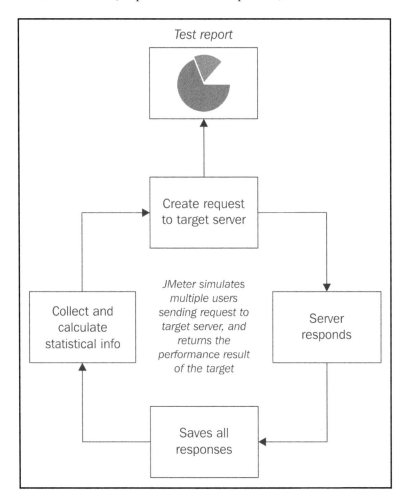

As you can see, this scheme is similar to the general performance testing process diagram that we've already shown, except for the first steps, as JMeter handles these responsibilities.

Fabric

Fabric is a mobile development platform developed by Twitter. This platform contains a really useful tool called **Crashlytics** (`https://try.crashlytics.com`). Figuring out why an application has crashed can be frustrating and complicated because you have to know how many of your users are affected and what the conditions were when the crash happened. Crashlytics was developed to help figure out why crashes occur. This tool accumulates crash reports and analyzes them to provide reports in the form of charts. Crashlytics helps developers focus on building great applications instead of detecting bugs:

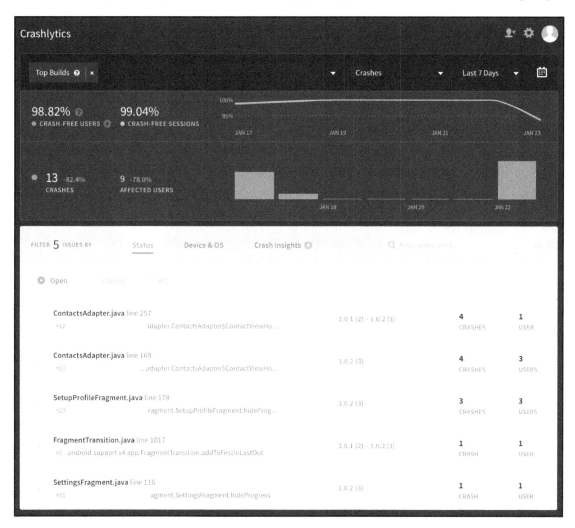

Summary

In this chapter, we presented the most common identifiers, tools, and approaches for detecting performance issues during testing and the post-release stage. We'll use these approaches in the following chapters. We also provided an overview of performance testing tools for different purposes and platforms, and talked about performance testing types before delving into benchmarking.

In the next chapter, we'll introduce different tools and profilers for identifying performance issues.

Learning How to Use Profiling Tools

3

By now, we have an understanding of what performance is. We also know which system bottlenecks lead to performance issues and how they do so. It's safe to assume that we're ready to talk about how to prevent these problems. It's much better to be proactive than reactive when it comes to potential problems, as the situation becomes much worse once the product has been released and is in the hands of actual users.

There are a lot of approaches and tools for detecting performance issues at the development stage. It's essential to detect these issues before releasing a product, and even before testing, because no one knows how your system works under the hood better than you. In this chapter, we'll talk about how to use various profiling tools, monitors, and viewers. We'll also observe how threads work, how much memory objects allocate, and how often the GC reclaims memory space.

In this chapter, we'll cover the following topics:

- Memory profiling
- Thread profiling

Memory profiling

In the previous chapter, we addressed bottlenecks that relate to memory management and the memory model. Now, we'll use the most common profiling tools to analyze the heap and detect problem places in code that can lead to performance issues. The easiest tool to use is **Memory Viewer** (`https://plugins.jetbrains.com/plugin/8537-jvm-debugger-memory-view`), which is built into IntelliJ IDEA.

IntelliJ IDEA, developed by JetBrains, is the most popular **Integrated Development Environment** (**IDE**) for Java software development. And naturally, since Kotlin is also primarily developed by JetBrains, IntelliJ IDEA has a powerful plugin to support Kotlin. That's why IntelliJ IDEA is also popular for Kotlin development.

Memory Viewer

IntelliJ IDEA has the Memory Viewer right out of the box, so you don't need to do anything to get started. This plugin extends the debugger and allows you to explore the heap during debug sessions.

The user interface of the Memory Viewer looks as follows:

Class	Count	Diff ▾
java.lang.Object	142	+6
char[]	1373	+4
java.lang.String	1359	+4
java.util.concurrent.ConcurrentHashM	159	+4
java.lang.Class	586	+2
java.lang.ref.Finalizer	149	+2
java.io.FileDescriptor	10	+2
java.io.FileInputStream	7	+2
Cup	1	+1

You can retrieve the following information using this tool:

- The total number of objects in the heap (grouped by class name for convenience)
- Changes in the number of objects between breakpoints

In this example, we'll use the following code snippet:

```
class Tea
class Coffee
class Cup<out T>(val drink: T)

fun main(vars: Array<String>) {
    val cupOfTea = Cup(Tea())
    val cupOfCoffee = Cup(Coffee())
}
```

We'll set up two breakpoints; one breakpoint is at this line:

```
val cupOfTea = Cup(Tea())
```

And the other breakpoint is at this line:

```
val cupOfCoffee = Cup(Coffee())
```

If you use the debugger in the **Debug** window, you can open the **Memory** window and search in it to find objects of a certain class, as shown in the following screenshot:

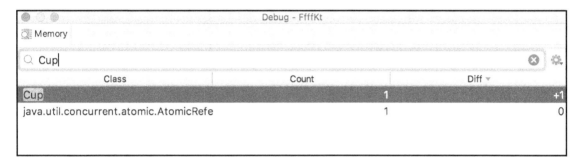

The preceding screenshot, which shows an example of a search, represents the state of the heap at the moment when the debugger reaches the second breakpoint. At this moment, the cupOfTea instance has already been created and the cupOfCoffee instance hasn't been created yet. In the **Count** column, we can see that the total number of objects of the Cup class is **1**. The **Diff** column shows that the difference in the number of objects between the current breakpoint and the previous one is **+1**. This means that one object has been created.

If you double-click on the row, a dialog window with all objects of this class opens up. Using this dialog window, you can look at the current values of fields or filter instances with a conditional expression:

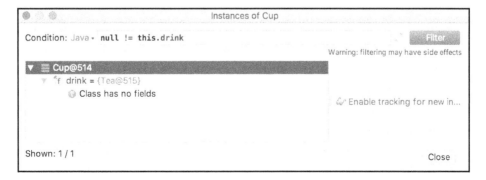

You can call the context menu from the **Debugger** window of any objects or fields to apply operations such as **Inspect...**, **Mark Object...**, **Set Value...**, **Copy Value**, and so on, to instances. This dialog window looks as follows:

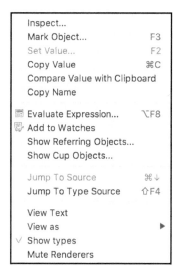

To perform deeper analysis, you can invoke heap dumping and retrieve a snapshot of the process in the form of an `.hprof` file.

HProf

HProf is a tool for profiling the CPU and the heap that's built into the JDK. HProf can generate files with the `.hprof` extension that contain detailed information about the current state of the JVM. HProf uses the bytecode insertion tool to get access to all class images that have been loaded into the JVM.

IntelliJ IDEA Ultimate allows you to generate a `.hprof` file in a simple fashion. All you need to do is click the **Capture Memory Snapshot** button in the **Tools** context menu:

A `.hprof` file will be generated and saved to the user directory as a `.zip` archive. After this, you can unzip the `.hprof` file. These are large files; in my case, it was 245 MB in size. The most common tool used to open `.hprof` files is the Eclipse Memory Analyzer tool.

Eclipse Memory Analyzer Tool

The **Eclipse Memory Analyzer Tool** (**MAT**) (`http://www.eclipse.org/mat/`) is a toolkit for analyzing heap dumps. It performs fast calculations of retained sizes and generates reports about leak suspects and memory consumption anti-patterns that relate to the `OutOfMemoryError` exception and high memory consumption.

MAT is a standalone application that requires only the BIRT Chart Engine (`http://www.eclipse.org/birt/`). If you already have the Eclipse IDE, you can install BIRT by going to the **Help** context menu and clicking **Install New Software...**:

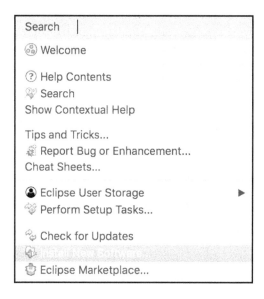

You can find a link to the latest version of BIRT on the BIRT Update Site (`https://wiki.eclipse.org/BIRT_Update_Site_URL`). Just paste the link shown in the following screenshot into the input field as follows:

In this dialog window, select all recommended items and click **Next**. Then, repeat the previous steps but with a link to MAT (`http://www.eclipse.org/mat/downloads.php`). After BIRT and MAT have been successfully installed, you can drag and drop the `.hprof` file into the Eclipse IDE. When you open the `.hprof` file, the **Getting Started Wizard** dialog window will open and will ask you to choose which type of report to generate.

The **Leak Suspects Report** is the simplest type, and it's enough for our purposes:

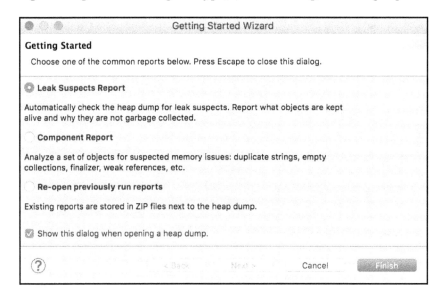

The **Overview** section of this report contains a pie chart that represents the biggest object by retained size. In our case, the chart looks like this:

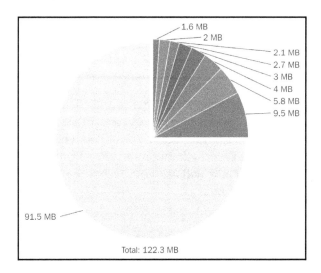

We can see that the total heap size is **122.3 MB**. The size of free space, shown in grey, is **91.5 MB**. The biggest part of the heap is allocated to the `com.intellij.util.lang.UrlClassLoader @ 0x7a0cbd970` object and is **9.5 MB**. You can retrieve class names of the biggest objects by pointing to the colored parts of the chart.

The bottom part of the **Overview** section contains the most common actions that can be applied to this memory snapshot:

Histogram

The **Histogram** table shows listed objects grouped by class name. You can sort the list by different parameters and analyze each group of objects. This table contains the following columns:

- **Class Name**: Shows the classes that were found in the snapshot
- **Objects**: Shows the number of objects for each class
- **Shallow Heap**: Shows the heap memory consumption of these objects
- **Retained Heap**: Shows the minimum retained size of these objects

The following screenshot is an example of what a Histogram table will look like:

Class Name	Objects ∨	Shallow Heap	Retained Heap
⚡ <Regex>	<Numeric>	<Numeric>	<Numeric>
© char[]	263,643	26,391,128	>= 26,391,128
© java.lang.String	261,976	6,287,424	>= 31,023,800
© java.lang.Object[]	87,230	6,648,424	>= 41,548,216
© com.intellij.util.SmartList	62,267	1,494,408	>= 3,441,328
© byte[]	57,929	9,760,144	>= 9,760,144
© java.util.HashMap$Node	55,158	1,765,056	>= 9,063,744
© java.util.concurrent.ConcurrentHashMap$Node	52,513	1,680,416	>= 12,974,120
© org.jdom.Attribute	49,916	1,597,312	>= 2,006,064
© com.intellij.util.text.ByteArrayCharSequence	49,166	1,573,312	>= 3,682,960
© java.lang.Class	48,685	293,504	>= 27,808,112
© java.util.ArrayList	47,707	1,144,968	>= 17,118,240
© java.util.LinkedHashMap$Entry	41,670	1,666,800	>= 2,789,176
© com.intellij.util.containers.IntObjectLinkedMap$MapEntry	37,036	1,185,152	>= 4,031,696
© com.intellij.psi.impl.java.stubs.impl.PsiModifierListStubImpl	32,632	1,305,280	>= 1,509,368
© org.jetbrains.kotlin.protobuf.SmallSortedMap$1	31,783	1,271,320	>= 2,069,080
© org.jetbrains.kotlin.protobuf.FieldSet	31,783	762,792	>= 2,831,880
© com.intellij.psi.impl.cache.TypeInfo	31,308	751,392	>= 788,712
© org.jdom.Text	30,194	724,656	>= 791,792
© org.jdom.ContentList	24,444	782,208	>= 3,594,208
© org.jdom.Element	24,138	965,520	>= 6,825,560
© org.jdom.AttributeList	24,138	772,416	>= 3,583,304
© org.jetbrains.kotlin.storage.LockBasedStorageManager$LockBa...	22,224	533,376	>= 10,130,608
© int[]	21,902	9,419,696	>= 9,419,696
© com.intellij.util.containers.hash.LinkedHashMap$Entry	20,213	808,520	>= 6,774,288
© org.jetbrains.kotlin.name.Name	19,621	470,904	>= 592,672
© org.jdom.Attribute[]	18,845	804,472	>= 2,810,648
© java.util.Hashtable$Entry	18,319	586,208	>= 1,896,696
© org.jetbrains.kotlin.serialization.ProtoBuf$Type	17,873	1,572,824	>= 3,668,352
© java.util.Collections$UnmodifiableRandomAccessList	17,804	427,296	>= 6,172,408
© com.intellij.psi.impl.java.stubs.impl.PsiClassReferenceListStubImpl	15,295	734,160	>= 857,768
© com.intellij.psi.impl.java.stubs.impl.PsiParameterStubImpl	14,929	716,592	>= 1,447,520
∑₊ **Total: 31 of 48,676 entries; 48,645 more**	**2,624,085**	**128,200,600**	

Shallow and Retained Heap

Depending on the operating system architecture, an object needs to be either 32 bits or 64 bits per reference. This is related to the machine word, which is a minimal fixed-size piece of data that can be handled by a given CPU's instruction set. The **Shallow Heap** is the memory consumed by one object.

We already know that one object can hold references to other objects. This is how a reference tree is created. And when the object, **X**, which holds references to others objects, becomes unreachable and unreferenced, then objects that are held by object **X** can also become available for the GC if no other objects hold references to them. The following diagram shows this:

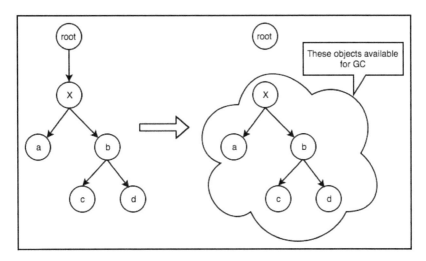

The set of objects, **a**, **b**, **c**, and **d**, represents a retained set of **X** that will be removed by the GC when **X** is garbage collected.

The **shallow size** is the size of one object from the retained set of **X**, and the Retained Heap of **X** is the sum of the shallow sizes of all objects in the retained size of **X**. Therefore, the **Shallow Heap** is the amount of memory that will be released if object **X** and its retained set are garbage collected.

Look at the second row of the Histogram table with `java.lang.String`. The **Retained Heap** column contains a value that's much bigger than the value in the **Shallow Heap** column. In the second row, we can see that if 261,976 objects of the `String` class, which takes up 6,287,424 bits, are garbage collected, then at least 31,023,800 bits of memory will be released.

Dominator Tree

A **Dominator Tree** is something like a transformation of a known reference tree. The name Dominator Tree was chosen because if, for example, object **X** holds object **a**, then object **X** dominates **a**. A Dominator Tree allows you to easily identify the biggest chunks of retained memory. The Dominator Tree has important properties:

- If **X** is the immediate dominator of **a**, then the immediate dominator of **X** also dominates **a**, and so on
- All objects that are dominated by **X** represent a retained set of **X**
- A Dominator Tree doesn't directly correspond to a reference tree

Here is an example of a Dominator Tree:

Class Name	Shallow Heap	Retained Heap ⌄	Percentage
⁺⁄₋ <Regex>	<Numeric>	<Numeric>	<Numeric>
▼ ⓞ com.intellij.util.lang.UrlClassLoader @ 0x7a0cbd970	80	9,961,488	7.77%
▶ ▢ java.util.Vector @ 0x7a0d826f0	32	9,044,736	7.06%
▶ ▢ com.intellij.util.lang.ClassPath @ 0x7a0ce0660	48	379,608	0.30%
▼ ▢ java.util.HashMap @ 0x7a0cbf288	48	274,120	0.21%
▼ ⓝ java.util.HashMap$Node[2048] @ 0x7a5275e48	8,208	274,072	0.21%
▼ ▢ java.util.HashMap$Node @ 0x7a0f140e8	32	824	0.00%
▶ ▢ java.util.HashMap$Node @ 0x7a0f14108	32	632	0.00%
▼ ▢ java.lang.String @ 0x7a17dd408 com.intellij.openapi.vcs.actions	24	104	0.00%
ⓝ char[32] @ 0x7a17d4f60 com.intellij.openapi.vcs.actions	80	80	0.00%
▶ ▢ java.lang.Package @ 0x7a133a698	56	56	0.00%
Σ Total: 3 entries			
▶ ▢ java.util.HashMap$Node @ 0x7a318d160	32	808	0.00%
▶ ▢ java.util.HashMap$Node @ 0x7a0f142a8	32	800	0.00%
▶ ▢ java.util.HashMap$Node @ 0x7a19d6a90	32	784	0.00%
▶ ▢ java.util.HashMap$Node @ 0x7a42410d0	32	752	0.00%

Top Consumers

The **Top Consumers** tab shows the important components that are using the most memory. Using the **Top Consumers** tab, you can get an overview of the biggest objects:

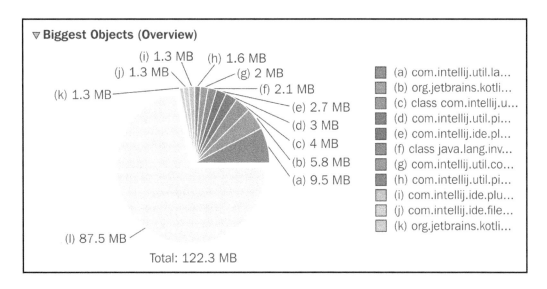

It also contains a list where you can find more details about a state of the heap:

Class Name	Shallow Heap	Retained Heap
com.intellij.util.lang.UrlClassLoader @ 0x7a0cbd970 »	80	9,961,488
org.jetbrains.kotlin.load.java.lazy.descriptors.JvmPackageScope @ 0x7a41e49c0 »	32	6,053,480
class com.intellij.util.io.CompressedAppendableFile @ 0x7a1ae7198 »	32	4,205,704
com.intellij.util.pico.DefaultPicoContainer @ 0x7a126fcc0 »	40	3,190,528
com.intellij.ide.plugins.cl.PluginClassLoader @ 0x7a32c45b8 »	96	2,813,472
class java.lang.invoke.MethodType @ 0x7a0d8d5b8 **System Class** »	56	2,210,944
com.intellij.util.containers.RecentStringInterner @ 0x7a3876360 »	24	2,084,200
com.intellij.util.pico.DefaultPicoContainer @ 0x7a4110150 »	40	1,713,152
com.intellij.ide.plugins.cl.PluginClassLoader @ 0x7a323fe28 »	96	1,472,296
com.intellij.ide.fileTemplates.impl.ExportableFileTemplateSettings @ 0x7a7515448 »	56	1,369,296
org.jetbrains.kotlin.load.kotlin.BinaryClassAnnotationAndConstantLoaderImpl @ 0x7a3314fa0 »	40	1,353,184
∑ **Total: 11 entries**		

This tab also contains information about the biggest top-level dominator classes/class loaders/packages.

Analyzing class loaders

Class loaders load classes into the Permanent Generation section of memory. The size of this section is also restricted, and the GC works with this section only during major garbage collection. There are different class loaders, and, as a result, the heap can contain duplicated classes. Therefore, it's important to explore class loaders when analyzing the heap. To get an overview of class loaders, you use the **Class Loader Explorer**, which shows loaders along with their number of defined classes and the number of created instances:

Class Name	Defined Classes ∨	No. of Instances
⧉ <Regex>	<Numeric>	<Numeric>
▶ 🔒 com.intellij.util.lang.UrlClassLoader @ 0x7a0cbd970	20,330	895,210
▶ 🔒 com.intellij.ide.plugins.cl.PluginClassLoader @ 0x7a32c45b8	9,263	396,375
▼ 🔒 <system class loader>	6,212	1,309,050
🄲 char[]		263,643
🄲 java.lang.String		261,976
🄲 java.lang.Object[]		87,230
🄲 byte[]		57,929
🄲 java.util.HashMap$Node		55,158
🄲 java.util.concurrent.ConcurrentHashMap$Node		52,513
🄲 java.lang.Class		48,685
🄲 java.util.ArrayList		47,707
🄲 java.util.LinkedHashMap$Entry		41,670
🄲 int[]		21,902
🄲 java.util.Hashtable$Entry		18,319
🄲 java.util.Collections$UnmodifiableRandomAccessList		17,804
🄲 java.util.concurrent.ConcurrentHashMap		13,779
🄲 java.util.LinkedHashMap		13,774
🄲 java.util.HashMap$Node[]		11,728
🄲 java.util.Collections$SingletonList		9,854
🄲 java.lang.Class[]		8,893
🄲 java.util.TreeMap$Entry		8,557
🄲 java.beans.PropertyChangeSupport$PropertyChangeListenerMap		8,459
🄲 java.beans.PropertyChangeSupport		8,426
🄲 java.util.HashMap		7,871
🄲 java.lang.Object		7,785
🄲 long[]		7,392
🄲 java.lang.String[]		6,781

To find duplicated classes, you can see the **Duplicate Class** table, which looks as follows:

Class Name	Count ⌄	Defined Classes	No. of Instances
<Regex>	<Numeric>	<Numeric>	<Numeric>
▶ java.lang.invoke.LambdaForm$DMH	384		
▶ java.lang.invoke.LambdaForm$MH	165		
▶ com.intellij.ultimate.PluginVerifier	15		
▼ java.lang.invoke.LambdaForm$BMH	7		
<system class loader> @ 0x0 System Class		6,212	1,309,050
<system class loader> @ 0x0 System Class		6,212	1,309,050
<system class loader> @ 0x0 System Class		6,212	1,309,050
<system class loader> @ 0x0 System Class		6,212	1,309,050
<system class loader> @ 0x0 System Class		6,212	1,309,050
<system class loader> @ 0x0 System Class		6,212	1,309,050
<system class loader> @ 0x0 System Class		6,212	1,309,050
∑ **Total: 7 entries**			
▶ com.intellij.Patches	2		
▶ com.intellij.ide.ClassUtilCore	2		
▶ com.intellij.ide.WindowsCommandLineProcessor	2		

Android Studio Memory Profiler

Android Studio is a special IDE for Android development. Android devices often have limited resources, and so profiling is important when you're developing for Android as you have to be careful with system resources. This is why Android Studio has a powerful profiler that can show a detailed timeline of your application's memory use and contains tools to force garbage collection, capture a heap dump, and record memory allocations.

Here's what the user interface of the Android Profiler looks like:

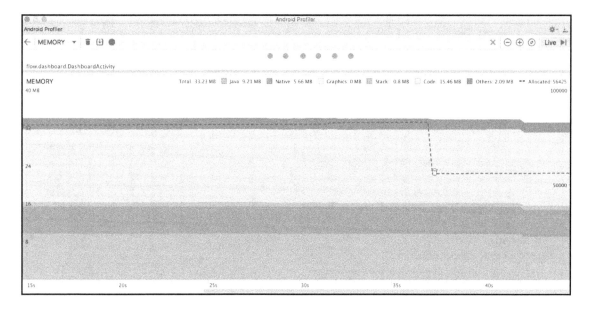

At the top, you can see buttons that allow you to perform operations:

- Force GC event
- Capture a memory snapshot
- Record memory allocations
- Zoom in/out of the timeline
- Start or pause live memory data mode

Purple dots mean that an activity state has just changed or a user input event or screen rotation event has occurred. The memory use timeline shows the following information:

- A stacked graph that represents how much memory is allocated to each memory category
- A dashed line that indicates how much memory is allocated by objects
- An icon that indicates a garbage collection event

Memory categories

The Memory Profiler divides memory into the following categories:

- **Java**: Memory allocated from Java or Kotlin code
- **Native**: Memory allocated from C or C++ code
- **Graphics**: Memory used by the graphics buffer queues to display pixels on the screen, including the **Graphic Library** (**GL**) surfaces and GL textures
- **Stack**: The amount of memory allocated by thread stacks
- **Code**: Memory that an application is using for code and resources
- **Other**: Memory used by an application but that the system can't categorize
- **Allocated**: The number of Java/Kotlin objects allocated by an application

The preceding mentioned categories are shown as follows:

Total: 36.88 MB ▦ Java: 11.93 MB ▦ Native: 5.48 MB ▢ Graphics: 0 MB ▦ Stack: 0.47 MB ▢ Code: 16.66 MB ▦ Others: 2.34 MB ▬▬ Allocated: 105385

Recording memory allocation

The Memory Profiler allows you to make a snapshot of the heap at some period in time. This feature is really useful if you want to know the following about the heap state:

- The class names of allocated objects
- How much space allocated objects use
- The stack trace of each allocation
- The moment when objects were garbage collected

You can use the record memory allocation and stop recording buttons to start and stop a recording session. Once you finish a recording session, a table with objects appears:

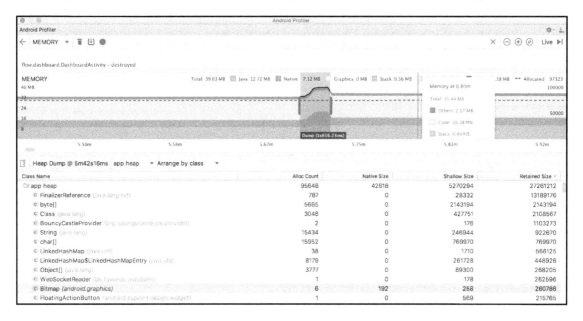

You can arrange this table:

- By class name
- By package name
- By callstack

You're already familiar with the concept of shallow and retained sizes so we'll briefly touch on the following columns:

- **Alloc Count**: The number of instances in the heap
- **Native Size**: The total amount of memory allocated from C or C++ code by objects of this class (for instance, in the preceding table you can see that instances of the `android.graphics.Bitmap` class allocate 192 bytes)

Using the drop-down list, you can also switch between the following heap dumps:

- **Default heap**: The initial state of the heap if the heap dump isn't specified by the system
- **App heap**: Your application's heap
- **Image heap**: Classes that are preloaded at boot
- **Zygote heap**: The heap that's used by the Android system to fork a new process for your application

 The Zygote is a process that starts during initialization of the Android system. This process allocates memory for common framework code and resources. When an application starts, the Android system forks the Zygote. The Zygote shares the allocated memory with the newly created process. This memory will only be copied if the new process tries to modify it. This means that the system stores all loaded core libraries in a single memory space because they're read-only.

You can click on the row to open the **Instance** window:

Instance	Depth	Native Size ▾	Shallow Size	Retained Size
Bitmap@320742064 (0x131e22b0)	10	32	43	75
Bitmap@320929120 (0x1320fd60)	9	32	43	201611
Bitmap@316786384 (0x12e1c6d0)	11	32	43	75
Bitmap@316786336 (0x12e1c6a0)	10	32	43	58875
Bitmap@316193184 (0x12d8b9a0)	10	32	43	75
Bitmap@317965648 (0x12f3c550)		32	43	75
mBuffer = {byte[]}		0	63504	63504
mDensity = 420		0	4	4
mHeight = 126		0	4	4
mIsMutable = false		0	1	1

The **Depth** column shows the minimal number of hops from the GC root to the selected instance. The **References** tab shows the list of references to this object. The **Bitmap Preview** tab shows a preview of the selected bitmap:

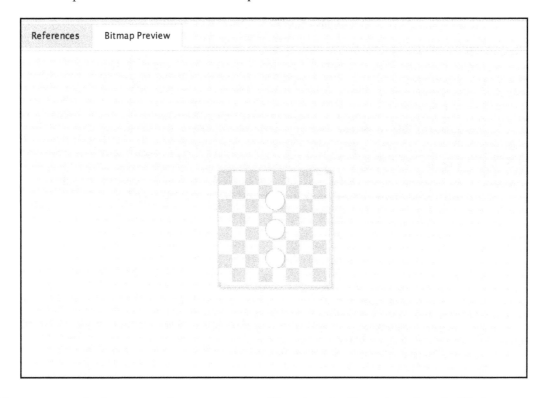

You can save the heap snapshot to a `.hprof` file using the **Export capture to file** button. You can then drag and drop this saved file to Android Studio to review the snapshot. The **Capture Analysis** tool allows you to detect memory leaks and find duplicate strings:

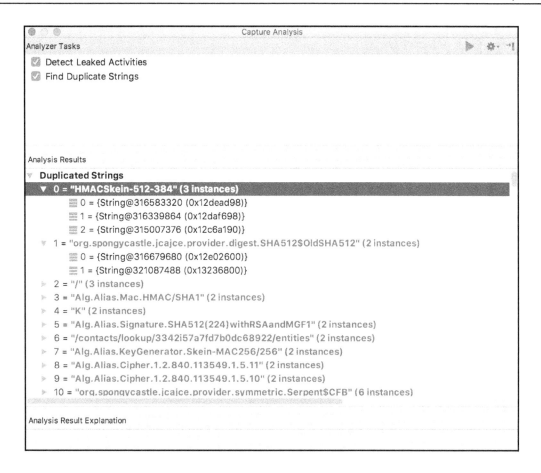

Threads profiling

To provide a faster and smoother user experience, you should care about CPU usage. Minimizing CPU usage preserves battery life and makes your application perform well on a mix of newer and older hardware. Thread profiling helps you find out which methods are executed over a period of time. You can also trace a call stack to identify a sequence of method invocations. You can use this information to determine which methods perform unnecessary work.

Threads viewer

The debug tools in IntelliJ IDEA have two very similar tabs—**Threads** and **Frames**. The **Threads** pane give you access to the list of threads that exist as of the current breakpoint. The **Frames** pane shows the current method or function that's being invoked. In this tab, you can get more detailed information about local variables. Let's return to our last example:

```
class Tea

class Coffee

class Cup<out T>(val drink: T)

fun main(vars: Array<String>) {

    val cupOfTea = Cup(Tea())

    val cupOfCoffee = Cup(Coffee())
}
```

We'll set a breakpoint at the line `val cupOfTea = Cup(Tea())`.

Frames pane

A **frame** represents something like a state of your program at a specific moment in time. It includes information about a current function that's been called and the values of local variables. The **Frames** tab looks like this:

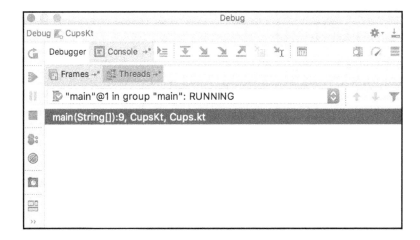

The **Frames** pane shows a method name, parameters, a line number, the name of a class, and the name of a file. You can choose the thread that you're interested in from the drop-down list:

The `Finalizer` thread is a daemon thread that runs an unterminated loop. During each iteration, the `Finalizer` thread checks whether a new object was added to the queue. The queue is an instance of the `java.lang.ref.Finalizer.ReferenceQueue` class. Objects are added to this queue when they become unreachable and unreferenced. If the `Finalizer` thread detects a new object in the queue, it invokes the `pop()` method and the `finalize()` method of the object. The `Finalizer` thread has low priority and gets less CPU time, which is why the `finalize()` method may not be invoked and some objects may not be garbage collected at this moment. The `Signal Dispatcher` thread passes the outcome signal to the appropriate component of the JVM when the operating system initiates it. The `Reference Handler` thread adds objects to the `ReferenceQueue`.

Depending on which thread is selected, the **Frames** pane shows information about the state of different methods:

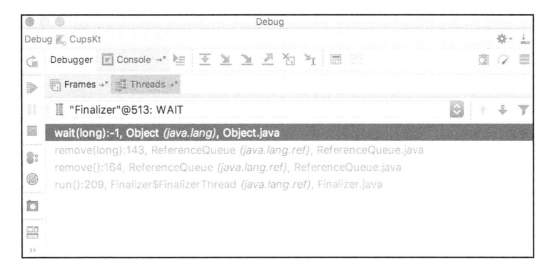

You can navigate between frames using buttons on the toolbar:

The Threads pane

The **Threads** pane focuses on threads and information about them. In the following screenshot, you can see the group, name, ID, and state of each thread:

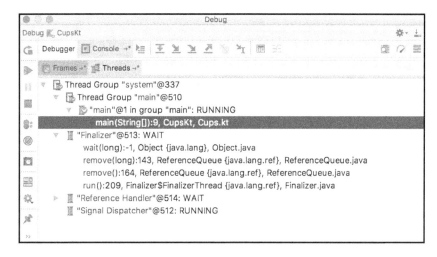

Using the context menu in the **Threads** tab, you can call the **Customize Threads View** dialog window:

Using this window, you can turn on/off whether certain information is displayed about a thread:

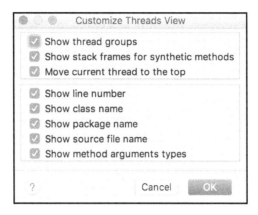

You can jump to the source code for a method by clicking on it in the **Threads** tab.

Thread profiling in the MAT

You're already familiar with the MAT and its use for memory profiling. The MAT provides several approaches to inspect threads using snapshots.

Threads Overview

The **Threads Overview** pane shows a list of all the threads from the heap snapshot. You can use the **Thread Overview** button or you can use the **Query Browser|Thread Overview and Stacks** query to open this pane:

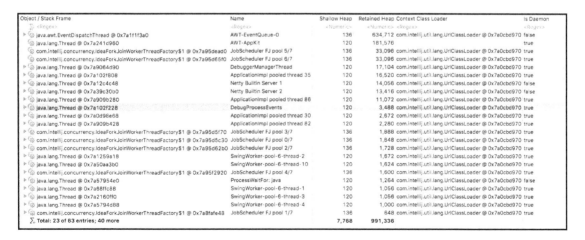

Here, you can see basic information about threads such as their name, **Shallow Heap**, **Retained Heap**, **Context Class Loader**, and so on.

Thread Details

You can call the context menu by clicking on a row and opening the **Thread Details** pane. The **Thread Details** pane gives more information about a certain thread:

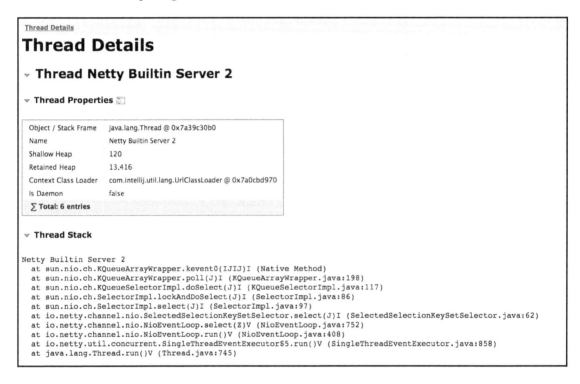

In the preceding screenshot, you can see a table with details about a thread and the **Thread Stack** pane showing the sequence of invoked methods.

CPU Profiler in Android Studio

The CPU Profiler displays the CPU usage and thread activity of your application. At first glance, it has a complex user interface, but it's an extremely powerful tool for identifying performance issues. When you open the CPU Profiler, you should see something like this:

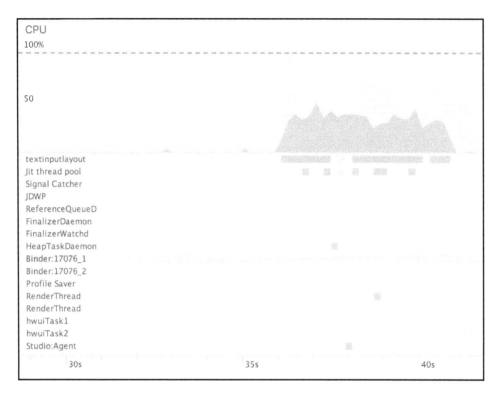

The bottom pane is the thread activity timeline, which shows a list of threads. You can inspect each thread individually by clicking on it. Each thread has a different color on the timeline that represents its current activity as follows:

- **Green**: Threads that consume CPU cycles or are ready to do so
- **Yellow**: Threads that are waiting for an I/O operation
- **Gray**: Threads that are sleeping

You can choose a recording configuration using the drop-down list in the top-left corner. This list lets you select one of the following options:

- **Sampled**: Your application's call stack is captured at frequent intervals
- **Instrumented**: The profiler records timestamps at the beginning and end of each method invocation; the profiler collects this data and analyzes it to generate method trace data
- **Edit configurations**: Lets you change settings in default configurations

The red circle button starts and stops recording a method trace. Once you stop a recording, the method trace pane appears, as shown in the following screenshot:

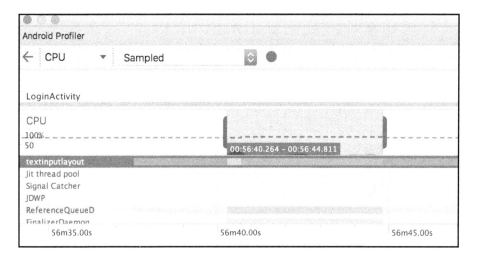

Here, you can see a selected time frame with timestamps that determine the portion of the recorded time that you've chosen to inspect. The trace pane displays the table with methods that were executed during this period of time. Using this table, you can find out the execution time for each method.

Call Chart and Flame Chart tabs

The **Call Chart** tab provides a graphical representation of a method trace. This tab shows the period of method invocation on the horizontal axis, which is color-coded as follows:

- **Green**: Methods that were invoked by your application
- **Blue**: Methods that were invoked by third-party APIs
- **Orange**: Methods that were invoked by the Android system

Call Chart	Flame Chart	Top Down	Bottom Up
main			
com.android.internal.os.ZygoteInit.main			
com.android.internal.os.Zygote$MethodAndArgsCaller.run			
java.lang.reflect.Method.invoke			
android.app.ActivityThread.main			
android.os.Looper.loop			

The **Flame Chart** tab shows the same information, only with an inverted call stack.

Top Down and Bottom Up tabs

These tabs display a list of methods that were called. You can expand a method to see the sequence from `caller` to `callee`. It's useful to determine a sequence of methods that are being invoked. It can give you a better understanding of your program workflow. The following screenshot shows that these tabs represent a sequence of methods being invoked as an expandable tree:

Summary

In this chapter, we presented the most common profiling tools and practices. Now you have all of the information that you need to debug, profile, and inspect code in your application. We introduced different profilers such as the Eclipse Memory Analyzer, the Profiler of Android Studio, and the Memory and Threads Viewer in IntelliJ IDEA.

In the next chapter, we'll inspect functional features of Kotlin and learn how Kotlin brings functional approaches to the world of JVM.

4
Functional Approach

It's clear to everyone that Kotlin is an object-oriented programming language. And its large number of built-in features makes Kotlin open to different paradigms. Particularly, Kotlin follows a functional style that brings a lot of new approaches that weren't available before for Java developers.

Object-oriented programming is ideally suited for modeling domains and representing real-world objects. Functional programming can elegantly pack a lot of actions into a few lines of code. Moreover, the concepts of immutable objects and pure functions from functional programming make scaling a program in a multi-core environment much easier.

Kotlin is a programming language that combines these approaches and lets you describe the behavior of objects flexibly.

In this chapter, we'll cover the following topics:

- Functional programming
- Inspecting functional features

Functional programming

Functional programming is a declarative programming paradigm that allows you to concentrate on the logic of a computation without describing its control flow. This is in contrast to imperative programming, which uses control statements to describe the flow of programs.

The following diagram represents a simplified classification of programming languages:

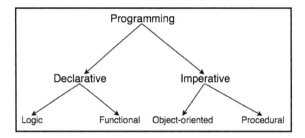

Functional programming assumes that the software is constructed based on the following principles:

- Pure functions
- First-class functions
- Higher-order functions
- Function composition
- Typeclasses
- Lambdas
- Closures
- Immutability

The following diagram shows a combination of these concepts:

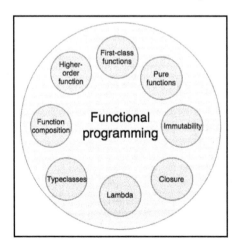

We'll look at some examples of declarative and imperative styles to get a better understanding. We'll cover all the principles of functional programming just mentioned.

Declarative versus imperative

The best way to explain the difference between declarative and imperative programming styles is to show examples. Let's assume that you need to write a function that retrieves only odd numbers from a list. If you write that code in an imperative style, it might look like this:

```
val numbers = listOf(1, 2, 3, 4, 5, 6, 7)
val odds = ArrayList<Int>()
for (i in 0..numbers.lastIndex) {
    val item = numbers[i]
    if (item % 2 != 0) {
        odds.add(item)
    }
}
```

This code describes the control flow in detail and contains a lot of statements. A statement is an element of imperative programming that describes some control action. Let's rewrite this code using a declarative style:

```
val numbers = listOf(1, 2, 3, 4, 5, 6, 7)
val odds = numbers.filter { it % 2 != 0 }
```

This code is built on expressions. An expression is something that takes parameters and produces a new value. For instance, it % 2 is an expression that takes two numbers and produces a new number, and it's combined with another expression, it % 2 != 0, that also takes two numbers and returns a Boolean.

Actually, Kotlin has more expressions than Java. For instance, when and if in Kotlin return values. Here's an example of if:

```
val max = if (a > b) a else b
```

And an example of when:

```
fun hasPrefix(x: Any) = when(x) {
    is String -> x.startsWith("prefix")
    else -> false
}
```

A declarative style allows you to concentrate on what to do instead of how to do it.

Pure functions

A **pure function** doesn't have any side effects, like input/output operations, and doesn't depend on a variable that doesn't belong to a scope of this function. This means that the return value of this function only depends on parameters that are passed to it. For instance, the Kotlin standard library has a special package called `kotlin.math` that contains mathematical functions and constants:

```
import kotlin.math.*

fun main(vars: Array<String>) {
    val minResult = min(3, 4)s
    val sqrtResult = sqrt(9.0)
}
```

This package was developed especially to support multiple platforms. Under the hood, these methods invoke other methods depending on the platform. If your program runs in the JVM, it calls static functions from the `java.lang.Math` class. You can see this if you open (`https://github.com/JetBrains/kotlin/blob/1.2.20/libraries/stdlib/src/kotlin/util/MathJVM.kt`) the `MathJVM.kt` file:

```
import java.lang.Math as nativeMath
....
@SinceKotlin("1.2")
@InlineOnly
public inline fun min(a: Double, b: Double): Double = nativeMath.min(a, b)
```

The value of `minResult` will always be the same for parameters 3 and 4. And the square root of `9.0` is always `3.0`. This demonstrates the most fundamental principle of functional programming, which considers computation as the evaluation of mathematical functions without a shared, mutable state. Pure functions allow you to write reliable and predictable code. You can just replace `min(3, 4)` with 3 and your program will work in the same way. The independent nature of pure functions makes code that is:

- Easy to test
- Easy to move around
- Easy to refactor or reorganize

To get a better understanding of pure functions, let's consider examples of impure functions. The following function is impure because its result depends not only on a parameter:

```
fun impure1(value: Int) = Math.random() * value
```

The result also depends on a value that is returned by the `random` function. This function isn't pure because it isn't predictable and returns a different result all the time.

Let's consider the following example:

```
class Person(val firstName: String, val secondName: String) {
    fun getFullName() = "$firstName $secondName"
}
```

The `getFullName` method isn't a pure function because it depends on variables that don't belong to a scope of the `getFullName` method. We can rewrite this method as follows:

```
fun getFullName(firstName: String, secondName: String) = "$firstName
$secondName"
```

And now `getFullName` is a pure function because it's predictable and its result depends only on arguments.

Using pure functions makes your programs more flexible and adaptable. It's an extremely powerful and reliable approach for developing applications that invoke parallel processing across multiple CPUs. Since a pure function returns the same value for the same parameters, the compiler can optimize and just replace the invocation of the function with the result.

The object-oriented paradigm considers everything an object. An object is a logical composition of several variables that represents a mutable state by means of methods. So to implement a pure function in Java, we have to use static functions. But Kotlin has a more elegant solution; first-class functions.

First-class functions

In computer science, first-class describes programming language entities that can be declared and used anywhere. For instance, a `class` with the `public` modifier is a first-class citizen in Java.

In Kotlin, you don't need to create a class to declare a function; you can just do it in the file. In the preceding sample, the `main` function is a top-level function that's just declared in the `Main.kt` file. It can be used as the starting point for a program because first-class functions compile to the same bytecode as `public final static` functions in Java. To ensure this, go to **Tools** in IntelliJ IDEA and the following dialog window will open:

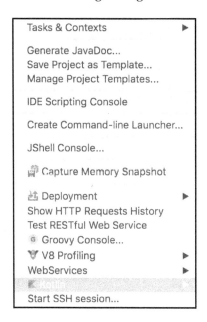

Go to the Kotlin submenu and click **Show Kotlin Bytecode** in the following context menu:

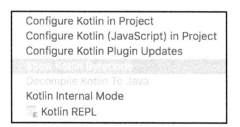

Now you can see the **Kotlin Bytecode** window:

```
                     Kotlin Bytecode
Kotlin Bytecode                                                        ⚙ ▾  →▌

            Decompile   ☑ Inline   ☑ Optimization   ☑ Assertions    IR    JVM 8 target

4    public final class MainKt {
5
6
7       // access flags 0x19
8       public final static main([Ljava/lang/String;)V
9         @Lorg/jetbrains/annotations/NotNull;() // invisible, parameter 0
10        L0
11         ALOAD 0
12         LDC "vars"
13         INVOKESTATIC kotlin/jvm/internal/Intrinsics.checkParameterIsNotNull (Ljava/lang/Object;Ljava/lang/String;)V
14        L1
15         LINENUMBER 11 L1
16         ICONST_3
17         ISTORE 1
18         ICONST_4
19         ISTORE 2
20        L2
21         ILOAD 1
22         ILOAD 2
```

This window allows you to inspect bytecode generated from Kotlin code. To get a more readable representation in Java code, click **Decompile**. The `Main.decompiled.java` file that contains the following code will be opened:

```java
public final class MainKt {
    public static final void main(@NotNull String[] vars) {
        Intrinsics.checkParameterIsNotNull(vars, "vars");
        byte var1 = 3;
        byte var2 = 4;
        Math.min(var1, var2);
        double var3 = 9.0D;
        Math.sqrt(var3);
    }
}
```

Now you have a powerful tool for inspecting bytecode and the Java version of your Kotlin code. We used this tool to ensure that first-class functions in Kotlin are compiled to the same bytecode as `public static final` functions in Java. First-class functions don't depend on some shared and mutable state, so they can be used to implement pure functions.

The first-class functions in Kotlin also support the concept of higher-order functions.

Higher-order functions

Functional programming tends to reuse behaviors, which are declared by functions, to process data. This trend has led to the creation of higher-order functions. In term of functional programming, a function is higher-order if it does at least one of the following:

- Takes one or more functions as an argument:

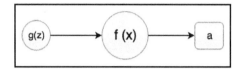

- Returns a function:

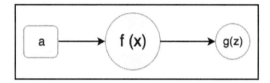

- Does both of these things at the same time:

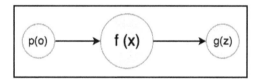

The most common example of a higher-order function is the map function:

```
public inline fun <T, R> Iterable<T>.map(transform: (T) -> R): List<R> {
    return mapTo(ArrayList<R>(collectionSizeOrDefault(10)), transform)
}

public inline fun <T, R, C : MutableCollection<in R>>
Iterable<T>.mapTo(destination: C, transform: (T) -> R): C {
    for (item in this)
        destination.add(transform(item))
    return destination
}
```

The following diagram shows how the `map` function works:

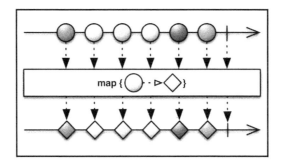

It's an extension function for the `Iterable` interface that takes the `transform` function as an argument, applies a transform for each element from the extended `Iterable` interface, and returns a list containing transformed items.

The `map` function is an explicit implementation of the strategy pattern. The main idea of this pattern is to be able to perform the same task using different algorithms during runtime. The `transform: (T) -> R` argument defines an interface that represents a family of algorithms.

The following example shows how we define a task that should be completed. During runtime, we choose a certain algorithm to use:

```
class Student(
        val firstName: String,
        val secondName: String,
        val age: Int)

val algorithm: (Student) -> String

when(someCondition) {

  age -> algorithm = { it.age.toString() }

  firstName -> algorithm = { it.firstName }

  else -> algorithm = { it.toString() }

}

val mappedStudents = students.map(algorithm)
```

Another common implementation of the strategy pattern is seen in the `filter` function:

```
public inline fun <T> Iterable<T>.filter(predicate: (T) -> Boolean):
List<T> {
    return filterTo(ArrayList<T>(), predicate)
}
public inline fun <T, C : MutableCollection<in T>>
Iterable<T>.filterTo(destination: C, predicate: (T) -> Boolean): C {
    for (element in this) if (predicate(element)) destination.add(element)
    return destination
}
```

The following diagram shows how the `filter` function works:

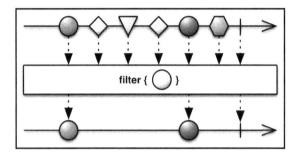

This function returns a list that contains elements that match `predicate`.

 A `predicate` is a statement that may be true or false depending on the parameters that are passed. It's also known as a Boolean-valued function and can be represented mathematically like this: `P: X-> {true, false}`.

The following example shows how it's used:

```
fun ageMoreThan20(student: Student): Boolean = student.age > 20

fun firstNameStartsWithE(student: Student): Boolean =
student.firstName.startsWith("E")

fun theLengthOfSecondNameMoreThan5(student: Student): Boolean =
student.secondName.length > 5

val filteredStudents = students.filter(::ageMoreThan20)
```

Let's imagine a case when we need to apply several filter conditions to a list:

```
students
        .filter(::ageMoreThan20)
        .filter(::firstNameStartsWithE)
        .filter(::theLengthOfSecondNameMoreThan5)
```

In this case, we have to invoke the filter function tree times. This decreases the readability of code and can lead to performance issues because each `filter` function is a loop under the hood. To deal with this problem, you can use a composition of functions.

Function composition

To solve the problem described in the previous section, we can just create a new method like this:

```
fun predicate(student: Student)
        = ageMoreThan20(student)
        && firstNameStartsWithE(student)
        && theLengthOfSecondNameMoreThan5(student)

students.filter(::predicate)
```

Or you can create the method like this:

```
students.filter(fun(student: Student)
        = ageMoreThan20(student)
        && firstNameStartsWithE(student)
        && theLengthOfSecondNameMoreThan5(student))
```

By using function composition, we can reach a more elegant solution like this:

```
students
    .filter(::ageMoreThan20 and ::firstNameStartsWithE and
::theLengthOfSecondNameMoreThan5)
```

Function composition is the combining of two or more functions to create a new function. It's a powerful approach for reusing functions. Function composition can be applied in different cases; for instance, to combine several invocations of the `map` function. Instead of this:

```
return prices
        .map(::discount)
        .map(::tax)
        .map(::aid)
        .sum()
```

You can write something like this:

```
return prices
        .map(::aid + ::tax + ::discount)
        .sum()
```

You can combine existing functions in different ways or assign a newly created function to a variable and reuse it:

```
val total = ::aid + ::tax + ::discount
val aidWithTax = ::aid + ::tax
val taxWithDiscount = ::tax + ::discount

prices.map(total)
prices.map(aidWithTax)
prices.map(taxWithDiscount)

val composed = total + aidWithTax + taxWithDiscount

prices.map(composed)
```

You can invoke a created function as a regular function:

```
val resultTotal = total(4.0)
val resultComposed = composed(5.4)
```

Function composition isn't implemented in the standard Kotlin library. But we can create our own functions; for instance, for combining predicates, you can use this function:

```
inline infix fun <P> ((P) -> Boolean).and(crossinline predicate: (P) ->
Boolean): (P) -> Boolean {
    return { p: P -> this(p) && predicate(p) }
}
```

And for combining functions that are invoked in a sequence, you can use a function such as:

```
inline operator fun <P1, R1, R2> ((R1) -> R2).plus(crossinline f: (P1) ->
R1): (P1) -> R2 {
    return { p1: P1 -> this(f(p1)) }
}
```

The repository with whole source code is available at: `https://github.com/ KucherenkoIhor/CompositionOfFunctionsInKotlin`. These functions are higher-order because they take and return lambdas.

Lambdas

In Kotlin, a lambda is a function that is decelerated without an identifier and the `fun` keyword, but with a certain type. Under the hood, a lambda is an object that has the `Function<out R>` type:

```
package kotlin
public interface Function<out R>
```

A lambda can take a varying number of arguments. To cover as many cases as possible, the `Functions.kt` file was created. This file contains 22 interfaces that extend the `Function<out R>` interface:

```
package kotlin.jvm.functions

public interface Function0<out R> : Function<R> {
    public operator fun invoke(): R
}

public interface Function1<in P1, out R> : Function<R> {
    public operator fun invoke(p1: P1): R
}

public interface Function2<in P1, in P2, out R> : Function<R> {
    public operator fun invoke(p1: P1, p2: P2): R
}
.....
```

The last interface looks like this:

```
public interface Function22<in P1, in P2, in P3, in P4, in P5, in P6, in
P7, in P8, in P9, in P10, in P11, in P12, in P13, in P14, in P15, in P16,
in P17, in P18, in P19, in P20, in P21, in P22, out R> : Function<R> {
    public operator fun invoke(p1: P1, p2: P2, p3: P3, p4: P4, p5: P5, p6:
P6, p7: P7, p8: P8, p9: P9, p10: P10, p11: P11, p12: P12, p13: P13, p14:
P14, p15: P15, p16: P16, p17: P17, p18: P18, p19: P19, p20: P20, p21: P21,
p22: P22): R
}
```

Look at the `plus` function from the previous section. It's an extension function for the `(R1) -> R2` type, which takes the `f: (P1) -> R` lambda and returns the `{ p1: P1 -> this(f(p1)) }` closure.

Closures

A **closure** is a function that has access to variables that are defined in the outer scope. In our example, the `{ p1: P1 -> this(f(p1)) }` closure captures the `f: (P1) -> R1` argument. Unlike in Java, variables captured in a closure can be modified in Kotlin. The following example shows how to modify a captured variable in Kotlin:

```
var totalAges = 0

students.forEach {
    totalAges += it.age
}
```

But in Java, this similar example will lead to a compilation error:

```
int totalAges = 0;

students.forEach(student -> totalAges += student.getAge());
```

The compilation error will read:

```
Error:(19, 49) java: local variables referenced from a lambda expression
must be final or effectively final
```

Typeclasses

A **typeclass** is a specification that defines some behavior that can be implemented for any class. It doesn't relate to inheritance or any other concept of object-oriented programming. You can consider typeclasses as object wrappers.

There are no typeclasses in the current version of Kotlin. But the **Arrow library** (`http://arrow-kt.io`) brings the most popular data types, typeclasses, and abstractions from functional programming to the world of Kotlin.

Arrow library

Arrow is a third-party library that contains popular abstractions, such as **Option**, **Try**, **Functor**, and **Monad**. You can use them to write fully functional code in Kotlin. The Kotlin standard library doesn't contain any abstractions from functional programming. You can use this library to bring more functional features to your project. The following list shows the main features of Arrow:

- Patterns
- Type classes
- Data types
- Effects
- Optics
- Integrations

> For more information you can check the following link: `https://arrow-kt.io/docs/patterns/glossary/`.

Let's look at the most popular typeclasses.

Functor

A **Functor** is a typeclass that can be mapped. You can consider it an interface that provides the map method to map one value to another. From an object-oriented programming point of view, it's a class that implements the Mappable interface. But a Functor is something that can be applied to any type, which is why, in Kotlin, the Functor is implemented as something like a wrapper class. The following diagrams show how it works.

Here's a simple value or an object:

Let's put the object into a wrapper that represents how the map method should be applied to objects of this type:

Now you can apply different functions to this object and the result will depend on the wrapper:

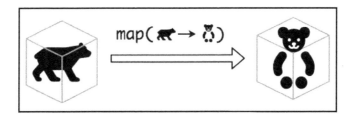

The preceding diagram demonstrates how a Functor actually works. The Functor has the map method that takes some function, for instance, transforming a bear into a teddy bear, and returning a new Functor. Each Functor has something like a context, and its result depends on this context.

The Arrow library contains the `Option` class. The simplified form of this class may look like this:

```
sealed class Option<out A> {

    abstract fun isEmpty(): Boolean

    fun nonEmpty(): Boolean = isDefined()

    fun isDefined(): Boolean = !isEmpty()

    abstract fun get(): A

    fun orNull(): A? = fold({ null }, { it })

    inline fun <B> map(crossinline f: (A) -> B): Option<B> = fold({ None },
{ a ->     Some(f(a)) })

    inline fun <P1, R> map(p1: Option<P1>, crossinline f: (A, P1) -> R):
Option<R> = if        (isEmpty()) {
        None
    } else {
        p1.map { pp1 -> f(get(), pp1) }
    }

    inline fun <R> fold(ifEmpty: () -> R, some: (A) -> R): R = when (this)
{
        is None -> ifEmpty()
        is Some<A> -> some(t)
    }

    inline fun <B> flatMap(crossinline f: (A) -> OptionOf<B>): Option<B> =
fold({ None }, { a -> f(a) }).fix()

    inline fun filter(crossinline predicate: Predicate<A>): Option<A> =
        fold({ None }, { a -> if (predicate(a)) Some(a) else None })
}
```

The `Option` is an abstract class that has two subclasses:

```
object None : Option<Nothing>() {
    override fun get() = throw NoSuchElementException("None.get")

    override fun isEmpty() = true

    override fun toString(): String = "None"
}
```

```
data class Some<out T>(val t: T) : Option<T>() {
    override fun get() = t

    override fun isEmpty() = false

    override fun toString(): String = "Some($t)"
}
```

The None object represents an empty state of Functor and the Some class represents a wrapper for some object. The Option class has methods for creating a Functor:

```
companion object {

    fun <A> pure(a: A): Option<A> = Some(a)

    tailrec fun <A, B> tailRecM(a: A, f: (A) -> OptionOf<Either<A, B>>):
Option<B> {
        val option = f(a).fix()
        return when (option) {
            is Some -> {
                when (option.t) {
                    is Either.Left -> tailRecM(option.t.a, f)
                    is Either.Right -> Some(option.t.b)
                }
            }
            is None -> None
        }
    }

    fun <A> fromNullable(a: A?): Option<A> = if (a != null) Some(a) else
None

    operator fun <A> invoke(a: A): Option<A> = Some(a)

    fun <A> empty(): Option<A> = None

}
```

Here's an example of how it's used:

```
class Bear(val age: Int)

class Teddy(val age: Int)

Option(Bear(5)).map { Teddy(it.age) }
```

The `DataTypeExamples.kt` file from the Arrow library contains examples of usage for other functions:

```
val someValue: Option<Int> = Some(42)
val noneValue: Option<Int> = None
....
```

Here are examples of using the `getOrElse` method to return a value of the `someValue` variable or a value that's returned by a function that is passed to this method:

```
someValue.getOrElse { -1 }.shouldBe(42)
noneValue.getOrElse { -1 }.shouldBe(-1)
```

These examples demonstrate the use of the `map` methods:

```
someValue.map { msg -> msg / 6 } shouldBe Some(7)
noneValue.map { msg -> msg / 6 } shouldBe None
```

The `fold` method extracts the value from an instance of the `Option` or provides a default, which is passed as a parameter if the value is `None`:

```
someValue.fold({ 1 }, { it * 3}) shouldBe 126
noneValue.fold({ 1 }, { it * 3}) shouldBe 1
```

Monad

Monad is a typeclass that has a single function, `flatMap`, and represents a sequence of executions. Let's use a new feature in Kotlin called multiplatform projects to create a small example.

First, create a standard Android project using Android Studio. Create the `android` directory and move the `app` module into it. All modules that relate to Android development will be located here. It's better to create a root `build.gradle` file with common configurations for all modules.

The structure of your project will look like this:

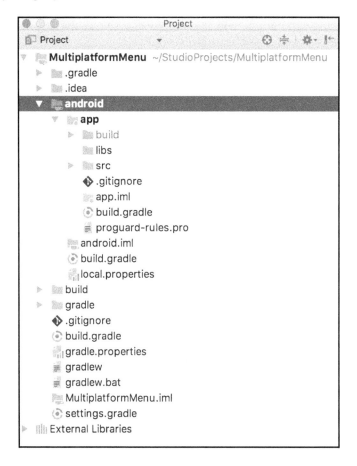

Gradle is an open source build automation tool that's used by Android Studio by default. The `build.gradle` file in the `android` directory looks like this:

```
buildscript {
    repositories {
        google()
        jcenter()
    }
    dependencies {
        classpath 'com.android.tools.build:gradle:3.0.1'
        classpath "org.jetbrains.kotlin:kotlin-gradle-
plugin:$kotlin_version"
    }
}

allprojects {
    repositories {
        google()
        jcenter()
    }
}

task clean(type: Delete) {
    delete rootProject.buildDir
}
```

Our project will contain the `backend` subproject and the `android` subproject. Both subprojects will have common code that will be located in the common module. We also have to create a common module for the JVM platform. So the structure of our project will look like this:

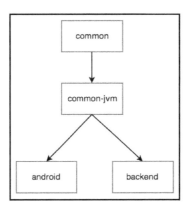

The structure of your project will now look like this:

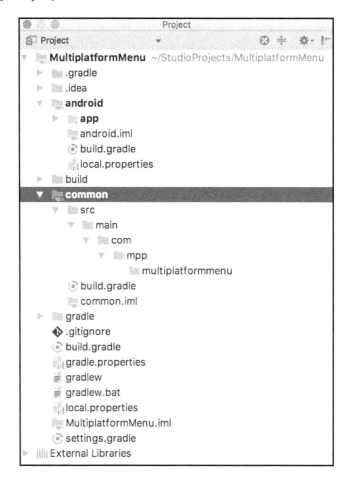

The `backend` subproject uses the `Ktor` framework (`http://ktor.io`) to build an API for clients. The common module contains the data package with the following classes:

```
data class Category(val id: Int = 0, val name: String)

data class SubCategory(val categoryId: Int, val id: Int, val name: String)

data class Item(
        val categoryId: Int,
        val subcategoryId: Int,
        val id: Int,
        val name: String)
```

These classes represent a restaurant menu that will be displayed to clients. The `backend` subproject contains a single class, `Server`, that looks like this:

```kotlin
val gson = GsonBuilder().setPrettyPrinting().serializeNulls().create()

fun main(args: Array<String>) {

    val server = embeddedServer(Netty, 8080) {
        routing {
            get("/categories") {
                call.respond(
                    gson.toJson(
                        listOf(
                            Category(1, "Menu"),
                            Category(2, "Drinks"),
                            Category(3, "Cocktails")
                        )
                    )
                )
            }
            get("/subcategory/{categoryId}") {
                call.respond(
                    gson.toJson(
                        listOf(
                            SubCategory(1, 1, "Salads"),
                            SubCategory(1, 2, "Fish And Seafood"),
                            SubCategory(1, 3, "Soups")
                        )
                    )
                )
            }
            get("/items/{subCategoryId}")    {
                call.respond(
                    gson.toJson(
                        listOf(
                            Item(1, 1, 1, "Overseas herring
caviar"),
                            Item(1, 1, 2, "Salted anchovy with
baked potatoes and homemade butter"),
                            Item(1, 1, 3, "Fried Anchovy with
Georgian sauce"),
                            Item(1, 1, 4, "Forshmak in a new way")
                        )
                    )
                )
            }
        }
```

```
    }
    server.start(wait = true)
}
```

You can start the server using the `./gradlew backend:run` command. Open your browser and go to this address: `http://localhost:8080/categories`. You'll see the JSON array as follows:

```
[
    {
        "id": 1,
        "name": "Menu"
    },
    {
        "id": 2,
        "name": "Drinks"
    },
    {
        "id": 3,
        "name": "Cocktails"
    }
]
```

The Android client uses the `Fuel` library (`https://github.com/kittinunf/Fuel`) for network operations. The Android client application will request the list of categories, take an ID of a first category in the list, and use this ID to request subcategories. After this, the ID of the first subcategory will be used to request items and display the list of items. The `API.kt` file will contain three functions to invoke these requests:

```
private fun getCategories(): IO<List<Category>> =
IO.pure(Fuel.get("/categories").responseObject<List<Category>>().third.get(
))

private fun getSubCategories(categoryId: Int): IO<List<SubCategory>> =
IO.pure(Fuel.get("/subcategory/$categoryId").responseObject<List<SubCategor
y>>().third.get())

private fun getItems(subCategoryId: Int): IO<List<Item>> =
IO.pure(Fuel.get("/items/$subCategoryId").responseObject<List<Item>>().thir
d.get())
```

So, we have a sequence of asynchronous operations. Let's look at some examples of how Monad can be used for this.

The first example looks like this:

```
try {
    launch(CommonPool) {
        getCategories().flatMap {
            getSubCategories(it.first().id).flatMap {
                getItems(it.first().id)
            }
        }.unsafeRunSync().let { items -> launch(UI) { adapter.dataSource =
items } }
    }
} catch (e: Exception) {
    e.printStackTrace()
}
```

This sequence of operations means that the getSubCategories function will not be called until getCategories returns a result. And the getItems function will be invoked if the getSubCategories function is successfully invoked. The application displays the result using the unsafeRunAsync method.

If you want to handle errors in another way, you can use, for instance, the unsafeRunAsync method, which provides a result wrapped in an instance of the Either class:

```
launch(CommonPool) {
    getCategories().flatMap {
        getSubCategories(it.first().id).flatMap {
            getItems(it.first().id)
        }
    }.unsafeRunAsync {
            it.fold({
                it.printStackTrace()
            }, {
                launch(UI) { adapter.dataSource = it }
            })
        }
}
```

You can use the comprehensions over the coroutines feature to avoid using the flatMap methods:

```
try {
    IO.monad().binding {
        val categories = getCategories().bind()
        val subcategories = getSubCategories(categories.first().id).bind()
        val items = getItems(subcategories.first().id).bind()
```

```
            items
        }.ev().unsafeRunSync().let { items ->
            launch(UI) {
                adapter.dataSource = items
            }
        }
    } catch (e: Exception) {
        e.printStackTrace()
    }
```

Monad is a type class that contains a `flatMap` method and can be very useful to combine several actions in one sequence.

Now you can run the Android client:

The full source code is available on GitHub (https://github.com/KucherenkoIhor/ MultiplatformMenu).

Immutability

The concept of **immutability** was described in the *Memory leaks* section of `Chapter 1`, *Identifying Performance Bottlenecks*. In Kotlin, all classes and methods are final by default. If you want to inherit a class and override methods, you have to use the `open` keyword. For references, you can use the `val` keyword, but it doesn't guarantee immutability. The following example shows a case when the `val` keyword doesn't work:

```
interface ValueHolder<V> {
    val value: V
}

class IntHolder: ValueHolder<Int> {
    override val value: Int
        get() = Random().nextInt()
}
```

In this example, the `value` property is read-only, but isn't immutable because the `get()` method returns different values all the time.

Since the popularity of Kotlin's multiplatform project feature is growing, it's important to know how to create an immutable object because immutability is the key concept of different architectures and frameworks. For instance, the concept of state from the *Redux* architecture is built on the `immutability`. Redux architecture and is based on unidirectional data flow. This architecture is very useful if your application contains a lot of components with a shared state that changes all the time and your components have to be updated whenever the state was changed.

Look at the following example in this repository (`https://github.com/brianegan/bansa`):

```
data class ApplicationState(val counter: Int = 0)

object INIT : Action
object INCREMENT : Action
object DECREMENT : Action

val reducer = Reducer<ApplicationState> { state, action ->
    when (action) {
        is INIT -> ApplicationState()
        is INCREMENT -> state.copy(counter = state.counter.plus(1))
        is DECREMENT -> state.copy(counter = state.counter.minus(1))
        else -> state
    }
}
```

The preceding example shows how functional features of Kotlin are well suited to implementing the Redux architecture.

The immutable object is an extremely powerful feature, but you have to understand that each modification creates a new object and makes the GC work more frequently. The following diagram shows this:

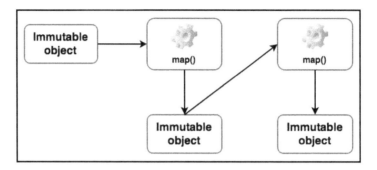

Inspecting functional features

Kotlin is a programming language that brings a lot of modern syntactic sugar features to the JVM world. These features increase a developer's efficiency, but they're compiled in the same bytecode as usual Java code. So it's better to know how the internals work so as to prevent unnecessary overhead.

You are already familiar with the Kotlin bytecode inspector, and it will be your main tool in this chapter.

Inline versus non-inline

Let's inspect the following code:

```
interface ValueHolder<out V> {
    val value: V
}

class IntHolder(override val value: Int) : ValueHolder<Int>

class DoubleHolder(override val value: Double) : ValueHolder<Double>
```

The `ValueHolder` interface uses a generic to be able to hold a value of any type. The bytecode for the `ValueHolder` interface looks like this:

```
public abstract interface ValueHolder {
    public abstract getValue()Ljava/lang/Object;
    LOCALVARIABLE this LValueHolder; L0 L1 0
}
```

The `getValue()` method returns an `Object` type because the compiler erases all generic types and replaces them with the first bound type. The first bound type is a type from which our generic extends. In the preceding example, the first bound type is `Object` because it's used by default. If a generic doesn't contain a bounded type, the compiler uses `Object` by default. To demonstrate this, the `ValueHolder` interface looks like this:

```
interface ValueHolder<out V: Number> {
    val value: V
}
```

Now, this interface allows classes that implement it to hold only subtypes of `Number`. The generated bytecode looks like this:

```
public abstract interface ValueHolder {

    public abstract getValue()Ljava/lang/Number;
    @Lorg/jetbrains/annotations/NotNull;() // invisible
    LOCALVARIABLE this LValueHolder; L0 L1 0
}
```

Let's look at the `IntHolder` class decompiled to Java code:

```
public final class IntHolder implements ValueHolder {
    private final int value;

    @NotNull
    public Integer getValue() {
        return this.value;
    }

    // $FF: synthetic method
    // $FF: bridge method
    public Number getValue() {
        return (Number)this.getValue();
    }

    public IntHolder(int value) {
        this.value = value;
    }
```

```
    }
```

It contains the `public Number getValue()` method. If you want to get a value from an instance of the `IntHolder` class, you'll invoke exactly this method under the hood instead of `public Integer getValue()`. So the `IntHolder` class contains three methods:

- Constructor
- Bridge method
- Getter for the value

Each class contains at least one method, as demonstrated here:

```
class SomeClass
```

The generated bytecode contains a default constructor, `public <init>()V`:

```
public final class SomeClass {
    // access flags 0x1
    public <init>()V
    L0
    LINENUMBER 72 L0
    ALOAD 0
    INVOKESPECIAL java/lang/Object.<init> ()V
    RETURN
    L1
    LOCALVARIABLE this LSomeClass; L0 L1 0
    MAXSTACK = 1
    MAXLOCALS = 1
}y
```

We already know that each lambda in Kotlin is an object that implements the `Function` interface. For instance, look at the `body: () -> Unit` lambda here:

```
fun main(args: Array<String>) {
    invokeBlock {
       println("body()")
    }
}

fun invokeBlock(body: () -> Unit) {
    try {
        body()
    } catch (e: Exception) {
        e.printStackTrace()
    }
}
```

This implements the `Function0` interface:

```
public interface Function0<out R> : Function<R> {
    /** Invokes the function. */
    public operator fun invoke(): R
}
```

Hence, a compiler generates one object that has three methods from the `body: () ->`
`Unit` lambda. To prevent the creation of extra objects and methods when using this
lambda, use the `inline` keyword:

```
inline fun invokeBlock(body: () -> Unit) {
    try {
        body()
    } catch (e: Exception) {
        e.printStackTrace()
    }
}
```

When decompiled to Java, the code will look like this:

```
public static final void main(@NotNull String[] args) {
    Intrinsics.checkParameterIsNotNull(args, "args");
    String var1 = "body()";
    System.out.println(var1);
}
```

The `inline` keyword tells the compiler to copy the body of the `invoke()` method instead
of invoking it. It's an extremely powerful feature, especially if you work with loops. Almost
all functions from the `Collection.kt` file are inlined, for instance, the `map` function:

```
public inline fun <T, R> Iterable<T>.map(transform: (T) -> R): List<R> {
    return mapTo(ArrayList<R>(collectionSizeOrDefault(10)), transform)
}
```

That's why the code looks like this:

```
fun main(args: Array<String>) {
    val ints = listOf(1, 2, 3, 4, 5)
    ints.map { it * it }
}
```

This compiles to something approaching the following:

```
public static final void main(@NotNull String[] args) {
    Intrinsics.checkParameterIsNotNull(args, "args");
    List ints = CollectionsKt.listOf(new Integer[]{1, 2, 3, 4, 5});
```

```
    Iterable $receiver$iv = (Iterable)ints;
    Collection destination$iv$iv = (Collection)(new
ArrayList(CollectionsKt.collectionSizeOrDefault($receiver$iv, 10)));
    Iterator var5 = $receiver$iv.iterator();

    while(var5.hasNext()) {
        Object item$iv$iv = var5.next();
        int it = ((Number)item$iv$iv).intValue();
        Integer var12 = it * it;
        destination$iv$iv.add(var12);
    }

    List var10000 = (List)destination$iv$iv;
}
```

This example shows that the compiler doesn't create an instance of the Function type and doesn't call the invoke() method in each iteration. Instead, it generates code that performs the body of the lambda directly inside the loop. But you have to take into account the fact that inlining leads to the growth of generated bytecode. The following example demonstrates this:

```
fun main(args: Array<String>) {
    val write = {
        val ints = listOf(1, 2, 3, 4, 5)
        File("somefile.txt")
                .writeText(ints.joinToString("\n"))
    }

    invokeBlock(write)

    invokeBlock(write)
}
```

If the invokeBlock is an inline function, the decompiled Java code can look like this:

```
public static final void main(@NotNull String[] args) {
    Intrinsics.checkParameterIsNotNull(args, "args");
    Function0 write = (Function0)MainKt$main$write$1.INSTANCE

    try {
        write.invoke();
    } catch (Exception var5) {
        var5.printStackTrace();
    }

    try {
        write.invoke();
```

```
    } catch (Exception var4) {
        var4.printStackTrace();
    }
}
```

But with the non-inlined `invokeBlock` function, the decompiled code will look like this:

```
public static final void main(@NotNull String[] args) {
    Intrinsics.checkParameterIsNotNull(args, "args");
    Function0 write = (Function0)MainKt$main$write$1.INSTANCE
    invokeBlock(write);
    invokeBlock(write);
}
```

Notice that in both cases, the `invokeBlock` function takes the same instance of the lambda. In bytecode, you can see that each class that implements the `Function` interface initializes a singleton in a static block to provide the ability to reuse this object:

```
// access flags 0x19
public final static LMainKt$main$write$1; INSTANCE

// access flags 0x8
static <clinit>()V
NEW MainKt$main$write$1
DUP
INVOKESPECIAL MainKt$main$write$1.<init> ()V
PUTSTATIC MainKt$main$write$1.INSTANCE : LMainKt$main$write$1;
RETURN
MAXSTACK = 2
MAXLOCALS = 0
```

Capturing and non-capturing lambdas

A **closure** is also known as a **capturing lambda** because it captures a variable from outside. Java doesn't allow captured local variables to be modified inside an inner-anonymous class or a lambda. This is because the lambda or instance of the inner-anonymous class can be passed to another thread, and if two threads can modify the same variable this can lead to a race condition. This restriction prevents multithreading issues. Kotlin allows you to modify a local variable inside a lambda:

```
fun main(args: Array<String>) {
    var counter = 0
    val inc = {
```

```
        counter ++
    }
    inc()
}
```

The decompiled Java code looks like this:

```java
public static final void main(@NotNull String[] args) {
    Intrinsics.checkParameterIsNotNull(args, "args");
    final IntRef counter = new IntRef();
    counter.element = 0;
    Function0 inc = (Function0)(new Function0() {
        // $FF: synthetic method
        // $FF: bridge method
        public Object invoke() {
            return this.invoke();
        }

        public final int invoke() {
            int var1 = counter.element++;
            return var1;
        }
    });
    inc.invoke();
}
```

Here, you can see that the captured value is held by an instance of the `IntRef` class, which in turn is referenced by the `final IntRef counter`. The `kotlin.jvm.internal` package of Kotlin's standard library contains the `Ref` class, which has nested classes similar to the `IntRef` class to hold values of all primitive types and objects:

```java
public static final class ObjectRef<T> implements Serializable {
    public T element;

    @Override
    public String toString() {
        return String.valueOf(element);
    }
}

public static final class ByteRef implements Serializable {
    public byte element;

    @Override
    public String toString() {
        return String.valueOf(element);
```

```
        }
    }

    public static final class ShortRef implements Serializable {
        public short element;

        @Override
        public String toString() {
            return String.valueOf(element);
        }
    }

    public static final class IntRef implements Serializable {
        public int element;

        @Override
        public String toString() {
            return String.valueOf(element);
        }
    }
    ....
```

In the generated bytecode, you can see that the inner class that's been created has a constructor that takes an instance of the IntRef class and a final reference to it:

```
// access flags 0x0
<init>(Lkotlin/jvm/internal/Ref$IntRef;)V
ALOAD 0
ALOAD 1
PUTFIELD MainKt$main$inc$1.$counter : Lkotlin/jvm/internal/Ref$IntRef;
ALOAD 0
ICONST_0
INVOKESPECIAL kotlin/jvm/internal/Lambda.<init> (I)V
RETURN
MAXSTACK = 2
MAXLOCALS = 2

// access flags 0x1010
final synthetic Lkotlin/jvm/internal/Ref$IntRef; $counter
```

That's why a new instance of Function is created all the time when you use a capturing lambda in your code. So, a capturing lambda isn't a cheap feature in Kotlin, and you have to be careful with it.

Summary

In this chapter, we presented the most common features of functional programming. We introduced pure functions, higher-order functions, and function compositions. We created a multiplatform project with a backend module and an Android client that uses the Monad concept to invoke a sequence of operations.

In the next chapter, we'll learn how to use collections in Kotlin.

5
Enhancing the Performance of Collections

A **collection** is an object that groups multiple elements into a single unit and provides an interface to perform various operations, such as sorting, insertion, searching, and deletion. The **Java Collection Framework** (**JCF**) provides a set of interfaces and implementations that cover the most common data structures. The standard Kotlin library extends the JCF to provide many methods for manipulations, such as `map`, `filter`, and `reduce`. Moreover, in Kotlin, collections are categorized as **mutable** or **immutable**.

In this chapter, we'll cover the following topics:

- Data structures
- Time complexity
- Collections in Kotlin
- Sequences in Kotlin

Data structures

A **data structure** is a way of organizing and storing data so that it can be accessed and modified efficiently. Data structures are built on the abstract data type model. This model represents an interface that's employed by a user to perform operations on data.

It's important to choose the right data structure for your task. The following list shows the most common data structures:

- Arrays
- Linked lists
- Stacks
- Queues

- Sets
- Maps
- Hash tables
- Binary search trees
- Tries
- Binary heaps
- Graphs

Arrays

An **array** stores multiple items of the same type in one fixed-size sequence. It's easy to access and modify any element of an array by referencing its index. Arrays are an efficient way of reducing the number of variables and grouping them by logic and type. In Java and Kotlin, a multidimensional array is an array of arrays; it can be used to represent matrices or some figures in space. You can create arrays with different depth levels, but it's hard to manage arrays with more than three levels of depth.

An array supports operations such as:

- get(index: Int): T
- set(index: Int, value: T): Unit

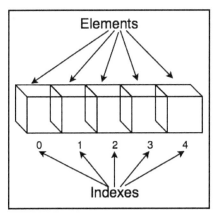

The algorithms of many data structures are built on arrays.

Linked lists

A **linked list** contains a group of nodes that represent a sequence. Each node, in turn, contains a link to the next node, as well as stored data:

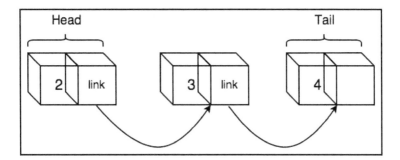

There are also doubly-linked lists, in which each node contains a link to the previous node in addition to the next:

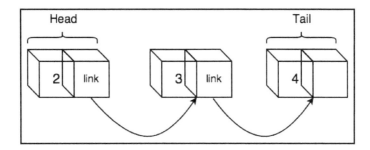

A linked list supports operations such as:

- `public E getFirst()`
- `public E getLast()`
- `public E get(int index)`
- `public E set(int index, E element)`
- `public void add(int index, E element)`
- `public boolean addAll(int index, Collection<? extends E> c)`

Stacks

A **stack** is a data structure that's built on the **last in, first out** (**LIFO**) principle and allows you only to insert or delete an item at the top of the stack:

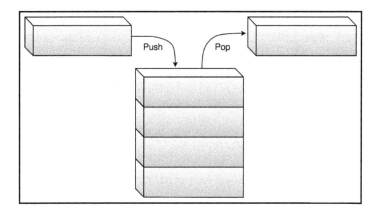

Once you're familiar with this data structure, we can get to the concept of the thread stack. Let's look at the following example:

```
fun main(args: Array<String>) {
    val value = 3

    blockTop(value)
}

fun blockTop(value: Int) {
}
```

When this program starts, a stack for the `main` thread is created. This stack will contain a block for the `main` function when the program enters the scope of the `main` function:

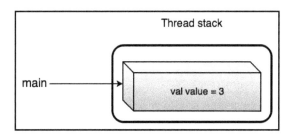

When the `main` function invokes the `blockTop` function, a new block is pushed to the stack:

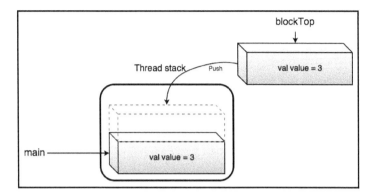

The `value` argument of the `blockTop` function is also created inside a new block as a local variable. After the push operation, the thread stack looks like this:

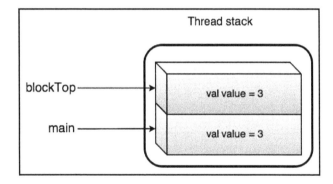

When the program exits the scope of the `blockTop` function, the `pop` operation is invoked:

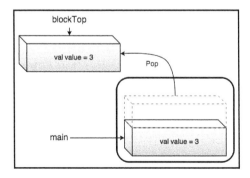

Queues

A **queue** represents the **first in, first out (FIFO)** principle. This means that after an element is added, it can be removed only after removing all other elements that were added before it. Unlike the stack data structure, you can manipulate items from both ends of a queue. A queue supports two operations—**Enqueue**, to insert element at the end and **Dequeue**, to remove it:

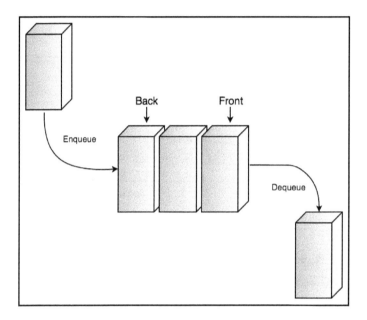

Sets

A **set** is a data structure that stores unrepeated values without any particular order. A common use of this data structure is to check whether a value or subset is included with a set or whether two subsets have common elements.

The most common operations on sets are:

- **Union**: Returns a new set that contains elements from two given sets without duplicates
- **Intersection**: Returns a set that contains all common items between two given sets

- **Difference**: Returns a new set of items that are stored in one set but aren't stored in another
- **Subset**: Returns a Boolean value that shows whether all items from one set, are contained in another

The following diagram shows the intersection operation:

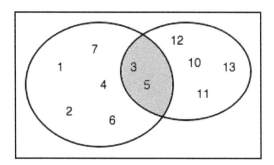

Maps

A **map** is a data structure that stores data in the form of key/value pairs. The map data structure is also known as an **associative array**. This is an extremely powerful data structure that provides you fast access to a value associated with a unique key.

A map data structure supports operations such as:

- `get(key: K): V?`
- `contains(key: K) : Boolean`
- `put(key: K, value: V): V?`

The following diagram shows the operation:

Key	Value
Shanghai	24 183 300
Beijing	20 794 000
Karachi	14 910 352
Shenzhen	13 723 000
Guangzhou	13 081 000

Hash tables

A **hash table** is built on a map data structure but uses a hash function to compute an index of items into an array of values. Since data in this data structure is stored in an associative manner, you can access a desired value very fast:

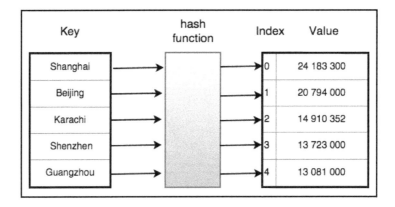

The `HashMap` class implements this data structure and supports operations such as:

- `open fun clear()`
- `open fun containsKey(key: K): Boolean`
- `open fun containsValue(value: V): Boolean`
- `open operator fun get(key: K): V?`
- `open fun put(key: K, value: V): V?`
- `open fun remove(key: K): V?`

Binary search trees

A **binary search tree** allows you find, add, and remove items quickly. Each node of this data structure has to be comparable. A typical implementation in Java or Kotlin assumes that a class that is used as a key implements the `Comparable` interface. To find a key, you have to compare the current node's key. If they are equal, then the root node is the result. If a key is greater than a current node's key, you have to move to a right node. Otherwise, you have to move to a left node.

It is built according to these rules:

- A binary tree has a root node.
- The left child node has a value that is less than the value of its parent nodes, and the right node has a value that is greater than the value of its parent nodes:

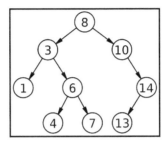

Tries

A **trie** data structure stores data step by step. Tries can be extremely useful for implementing autocomplete. Unlike a binary search tree, the position of the node in the tree defines the key with which it is associated. Usually, a string is used as a key for this data structure. The Kotlin standard library and JDK don't contain an implementation of this data structure:

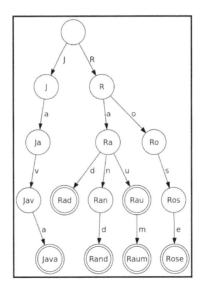

The cost of searching for a word or prefix is fixed and depends only on the number of characters.

Binary heaps

Each node of a binary heap has no more than two children. In a **binary heap**, the order of levels is important, but the order of values at the same level isn't important. There are two types of binary heaps—**max** and **min**. A max binary heap places the largest value in the top node, and a min binary heap places it in the bottom node.

The following diagram shows a max heap:

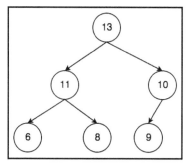

This diagram shows a min heap:

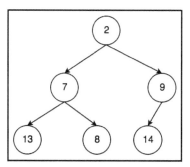

Graphs

Graphs are collections of nodes (also called **vertices**) and the connections (called **edges**) between them. Graphs are also known as **networks**. One example of a graph is a social network. In a social network, nodes are people and edges are friendships.

There are two types of graphs:

- Directed
- Undirected

The following diagram shows a directed graph:

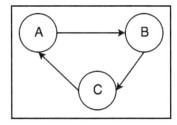

And this diagram shows an undirected graph:

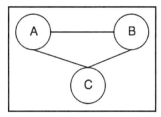

Time complexity

Time complexity measures, or estimates, the time by counting the number of elementary operations. It assumes that performing an elementary operation takes a fixed amount of time. To get a fixed amount of time, you can assume either worst-case complexity or average complexity.

Most commonly, the big **O** notation is used to express time complexity; for instance, **O(1)** or **O(n)**:

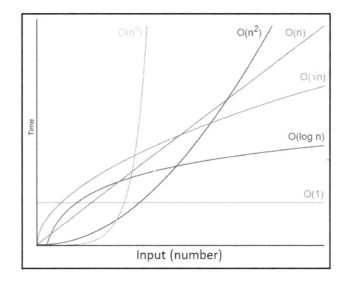

Let's look at the time complexity of the collections from the JDK.

Calculating time complexity

Let's look at the next example:

```
inline fun operation(n: Int, statement: () -> Unit) {
    for (i in 0..n) {
        statement()
    }
}
```

The execution time of the statement is constant. The time complexity of the preceding code is linear, or **O(n)** if we're using big **O** notation. We can rewrite the operation function as follows:

```
inline fun operation(n: Int, statement: () -> Unit) {
    for (i in 0..n) {
        for (k in 0..n) {
            statement()
        }
    }
}
```

When we do, we'll get a quadratic time complexity that can be expressed like this—**O(n*n)**.

Time complexity of lists

The following table shows the time complexity of the most common list operations:

Add	Remove	Get	Contains	Data structure	
ArrayList	O(1)	O(n)	O(1)	O(n)	Array
LinkedList	O(1)	O(1)	O(n)	O(n)	Linked list
CopyOnWriteArrayList	O(n)	O(n)	O(1)	O(n)	Array

The `java.util.concurrent` package includes special collections, such as `CopyOnWriteArrayList` or `ConcurrentSkipListSet`, that help you to avoid errors when different threads have inconsistent views of data that's stored in the same variable. These collections have similar public methods as regular collections, but can be used safely in multithreaded environments.

Time complexity of sets

The following table shows the time complexity of the most common set operations:

	Add	Contains	Next	Data structure
HashSet	O(1)	O(1)	O(h/n)	Hash table
LinkedHashSet	O(1)	O(1)	O(1)	Hash table + linked list
EnumSet	O(1)	O(1)	O(1)	Bit vector
TreeSet	O(log n)	O(log n)	O(log n)	Red-black tree
CopyOnWriteArraySet	O(n)	O(n)	O(1)	Array

ConcurrentSkipListSet	O(log n)	O(log n)	O(1)	Skip list

Time complexity of queues

The following table shows the time complexity of the most common queue operations:

	Offer	Peek	Poll	Size	Data structure
PriorityQueue	O(log n)	O(1)	O(log n)	O(1)	Priority heap
LinkedList	O(1)	O(1)	O(1)	O(1)	Array
ArrayDequeue	O(1)	O(1)	O(1)	O(1)	Linked list
ConcurrentLinkedQueue	O(1)	O(1)	O(1)	O(n)	Linked list
ArrayBlockingQueue	O(1)	O(1)	O(1)	O(1)	Array
PriorirityBlockingQueue	O(log n)	O(1)	O(log n)	O(1)	Priority heap
SynchronousQueue	O(1)	O(1)	O(1)	O(1)	None!
DelayQueue	O(log n)	O(1)	O(log n)	O(1)	Priority heap
LinkedBlockingQueue	O(1)	O(1)	O(1)	O(1)	Linked list

Time complexity of maps

The following table shows the time complexity of the most common map operations:

	Get	ContainsKey	Next	Data structure
HashMap	O(1)	O(1)	O(h / n)	Hash table
LinkedHashMap	O(1)	O(1)	O(1)	Hash table + linked list
IdentityHashMap	O(1)	O(1)	O(h / n)	Array
WeakHashMap	O(1)	O(1)	O(h / n)	Hash table
EnumMap	O(1)	O(1)	O(1)	Array

TreeMap	O(log n)	O(log n)	O(log n)	Red-black tree
ConcurrentHashMap	O(1)	O(1)	O(h / n)	Hash tables
ConcurrentSkipListMap	O(log n)	O(log n)	O(1)	Skip list

Collections in Kotlin

Kotlin has both mutable and immutable collections. Having implicit control over whether collections can be edited is useful for writing clear and reliable code. It's important to understand that immutable collections in Kotlin are simply read-only, as the JVM doesn't see a difference between an immutable and mutable collection.

Let's look at the simplified version of the `Collections.kt` file:

```
public fun <T> emptyList(): List<T> = EmptyList

public fun <T> listOf(vararg elements: T): List<T> = if (elements.size > 0)
elements.asList() else emptyList()

public inline fun <T> listOf(): List<T> = emptyList()

public fun <T> listOf(element: T): List<T> =
java.util.Collections.singletonList(element)

public inline fun <T> mutableListOf(): MutableList<T> = ArrayList()

public inline fun <T> arrayListOf(): ArrayList<T> = ArrayList()

public fun <T> mutableListOf(vararg elements: T): MutableList<T>
        = if (elements.size == 0) ArrayList() else
ArrayList(ArrayAsCollection(elements, isVarargs = true))

public fun <T> arrayListOf(vararg elements: T): ArrayList<T>
        = if (elements.size == 0) ArrayList() else
ArrayList(ArrayAsCollection(elements, isVarargs = true))

public fun <T : Any> listOfNotNull(element: T?): List<T> = if (element !=
null) listOf(element) else emptyList()
```

And the `Maps.kt` file:

```
public fun <K, V> emptyMap(): Map<K, V> = @Suppress("UNCHECKED_CAST")
(EmptyMap as Map<K, V>)

public fun <K, V> mapOf(vararg pairs: Pair<K, V>): Map<K, V> = if
(pairs.size > 0) pairs.toMap(LinkedHashMap(mapCapacity(pairs.size))) else
emptyMap()

public inline fun <K, V> mapOf(): Map<K, V> = emptyMap()

public inline fun <K, V> mutableMapOf(): MutableMap<K, V> = LinkedHashMap()

public fun <K, V> mutableMapOf(vararg pairs: Pair<K, V>): MutableMap<K, V>
        = LinkedHashMap<K, V>(mapCapacity(pairs.size)).apply {
putAll(pairs) }

public inline fun <K, V> hashMapOf(): HashMap<K, V> = HashMap<K, V>()
```

And the `Sets.kt` file:

```
public inline fun <T> setOf(): Set<T> = emptySet()

public fun <T> setOf(vararg elements: T): Set<T> = if (elements.size > 0)
elements.toSet() else emptySet()

public fun <T> emptySet(): Set<T> = EmptySet

public inline fun <T> mutableSetOf(): MutableSet<T> = LinkedHashSet()

public fun <T> mutableSetOf(vararg elements: T): MutableSet<T> =
elements.toCollection(LinkedHashSet(mapCapacity(elements.size)))

public fun <T> hashSetOf(vararg elements: T): HashSet<T> =
elements.toCollection(HashSet(mapCapacity(elements.size)))

public inline fun <T> linkedSetOf(): LinkedHashSet<T> = LinkedHashSet()
```

Now you have an understanding of what type of collection will be created when you use a certain function. This is important to know because different implementations use different methods with different invocation times.

The `_Collections.kt` file contains many useful functions for data processing. For instance, `forEach`:

```
students.forEach {
    println(it.firstName)
}
```

When we decompile this code to Java, we can see that the Kotlin compiler uses `Iterator` under the hood:

```
Iterable $receiver$iv = (Iterable)MyBenchmarkKt.getStudents();
Iterator var2 = $receiver$iv.iterator();

while(var2.hasNext()) {
    Object element$iv = var2.next();
    Student it = (Student)element$iv;
    String var5 = it.getFirstName();
    System.out.println(var5);
}
```

We can create our own implementation of `forEach`:

```
inline fun <reified T> List<T>.foreach(crossinline invoke: (T) -> Unit):
Unit {
    val size = size
    var i = 0
    while (i < size) {
        invoke(get(i))
        i ++
    }
}
```

We can also qualify the `type` parameter to make it accessible inside a function.

Let's run benchmarks to compare the execution times of the `forEach` and `foreach` methods:

```
@Benchmark
fun forEachIterator() {
    students.forEach {
        println(it.firstName)
    }
}

@Benchmark
fun forEachWhile() {
```

```
    students.foreach {
        println(it.firstName)
    }
}
```

Here's the result:

```
Benchmark Mode                      Score        Error      Units
MyBenchmark.forEachIterator    292255.882 ± 33821.268  ns/op
MyBenchmark.forEachWhile       181588.728 ±  2358.050  ns/op
```

As you can see, the `foreach` function with `while` is the fastest and you should consider creating your own `foreach` method.

The `students` list was created using the `listOf` function, which creates an instance of `ArrayList` under the hood. Let's run the same benchmarks, but with `LinkedList`:

```
@Benchmark
fun forEachIterator() {
    LinkedList<Student>(students).forEach {
        println(it.firstName)
    }
}

@Benchmark
fun forEachWhile() {
    LinkedList<Student>(students).foreach {
        println(it.firstName)
    }
}
```

Here's the result:

```
Benchmark            Score        Error     Units
forEachIterator  151212.682 ± 2068.069   ns/op
forEachWhile     166874.210 ± 7877.704   ns/op
```

There's no essential difference between the benchmarked times of the `forEachIterator` and `forEachWhile` methods, so you can simply always use the default `forEach` method when you work without `ArrayList`.

Sequences in Kotlin

Java 8 introduced lazy evaluation for collections using the Stream API. Kotlin has a similar feature called `Sequence`. The API of the `Sequence` class is similar to the API of the `List` class. But from the point of view of the return type, `Sequence` methods class can be classified into the following groups:

- Intermediate
- Terminal

Intermediate methods return an instance of the `Sequence` class and **terminal** methods return an instance of the `List` class. The `Sequence` class actually starts to perform evaluations when meeting the `terminal` operator.

To create an instance of the `Sequence` class, you can just invoke the `asSequence()` method on a `list` or `range`:

```
(0..1_000_000)
      .asSequence()
```

This method looks as follows:

```
public fun <T> Iterable<T>.asSequence(): Sequence<T> {
    return Sequence { this.iterator() }
}
```

`Sequence` is a method that creates a new instance of the `Sequence` class:

```
public inline fun <T> Sequence(crossinline iterator: () -> Iterator<T>):
Sequence<T> = object : Sequence<T> {
    override fun iterator(): Iterator<T> = iterator()
}
```

`Sequence` is an interface that looks like this:

```
public interface Sequence<out T> {
    public operator fun iterator(): Iterator<T>
}
```

Let's write and inspect the `benchmark` methods, as follows:

```
@Benchmark
fun list() = (0..1_000_000)
        .filter { it % 2 == 0 }
        .map { it * it }
        .first()

@Benchmark
fun sequence() = (0..1_000_000)
        .asSequence()
        .filter { it % 2 == 0 }
        .map { it * it }
        .first()
```

The decompiled version of the `sequence` method looks like this:

```
@Benchmark
public final int sequence() {
   byte var1 = 0;
   return
((Number)SequencesKt.first(SequencesKt.map(SequencesKt.filter(CollectionsKt
.asSequence((Iterable)(new IntRange(var1, 1000000)))),
(Function1)null.INSTANCE), (Function1)null.INSTANCE))).intValue();
}
```

The `SequencesKt` file contains extension functions for the `Sequence` class:

```
public fun <T> Sequence<T>.filter(predicate: (T) -> Boolean): Sequence<T> {
    return FilteringSequence(this, true, predicate)
}
```

The `FilteringSequence` class looks as follows:

```
internal class FilteringSequence<T>(private val sequence: Sequence<T>,
                                    private val sendWhen: Boolean = true,
                                    private val predicate: (T) -> Boolean
                                    ) : Sequence<T> {

    override fun iterator(): Iterator<T> = object : Iterator<T> {
        val iterator = sequence.iterator()
        var nextState: Int = -1 // -1 for unknown, 0 for done, 1 for
continue
        var nextItem: T? = null

        private fun calcNext() {
            while (iterator.hasNext()) {
                val item = iterator.next()
```

```
                    if (predicate(item) == sendWhen) {
                        nextItem = item
                        nextState = 1
                        return
                    }
                }
                nextState = 0
            }

        override fun next(): T {
            if (nextState == -1)
                calcNext()
            if (nextState == 0)
                throw NoSuchElementException()
            val result = nextItem
            nextItem = null
            nextState = -1
            @Suppress("UNCHECKED_CAST")
            return result as T
        }

        override fun hasNext(): Boolean {
            if (nextState == -1)
                calcNext()
            return nextState == 1
        }
    }
}
}
```

This class implements the `Sequence` interface and overrides the `iterator` method, using an instance of `Iterator` from the sequence argument.

The `map` extension method returns an instance of the `TransformingSequence` class:

```
public fun <T, R> Sequence<T>.map(transform: (T) -> R): Sequence<R> {
    return TransformingSequence(this, transform)
}
```

The `TransformingSequence` class looks as follows:

```
internal class TransformingSequence<T, R>
constructor(private val sequence: Sequence<T>, private val transformer: (T)
-> R) : Sequence<R> {
    override fun iterator(): Iterator<R> = object : Iterator<R> {
        val iterator = sequence.iterator()
        override fun next(): R {
            return transformer(iterator.next())
```

```
        }

        override fun hasNext(): Boolean {
            return iterator.hasNext()
        }
    }

    internal fun <E> flatten(iterator: (R) -> Iterator<E>): Sequence<E> {
        return FlatteningSequence<T, R, E>(sequence, transformer, iterator)
    }
}
```

This class also reuses an instance of `iterator` from the passed `Sequence`.

So, a `sequence` value uses one instance of the `Iterator` for all operations, and we have just one loop instead of several `while` loops.

Here's the result of our benchmarks:

```
Benchmark        Score            Error           Units
list             8843807.556 ± 75472.233          ns/op
sequence         28.591       ± 0.181             ns/op
```

The source code of the `first()` method looks like this:

```
public fun <T> Sequence<T>.first(): T {
    val iterator = iterator()
    if (!iterator.hasNext())
        throw NoSuchElementException("Sequence is empty.")
    return iterator.next()
}
```

As we can see, using sequences can increase performance significantly.

Summary

In this chapter, we introduced data structures, time complexity, and collections and sequences in Kotlin. We used the JMH framework to inspect code and found some approaches to improve the performance of various operations.

In the next chapter, we'll learn how to optimize access to fields in Kotlin.

6
Optimizing Access to Properties

Properties are class members that hold values and define rules for reading and writing those values. In Kotlin, the properties of a class represent the current state of an instance of that class. A typical class with properties looks like this:

```
class Button {

    var text: String = TODO()

    var backgroundColor: Int = TODO()
    var onClickListener: ((Button) -> Unit)? = null

}
```

We can use this class to create objects and set values for the `text`, `backgroundColor`, and `onClickListener` properties. A combination of these properties in one object represents the state of an instance of the `Button` class.

In this chapter, we'll cover the following topics:

- Fields and properties

- Code inspection

Fields and properties

In the preceding example, I used a special function, `TODO()`, from the Kotlin standard library. This function is overloaded and has two implementations:

```
@kotlin.internal.InlineOnly
public inline fun TODO(): Nothing = throw NotImplementedError()

@kotlin.internal.InlineOnly
```

```
public inline fun TODO(reason: String): Nothing = throw
NotImplementedError("An operation is not implemented: $reason")
```

It's very useful when you're modeling a class and don't want to implement certain class members right away. You can also use it for methods, as shown in the following code:

```
fun click() {
    TODO()
}
```

And you can use it for constructors as well:

```
constructor() {
    TODO()
}
```

Let's look at how the Button class decompiled to Java:

```
public final class Button {
    @NotNull
    private String text;
    private int backgroundColor;
    @Nullable
    private Function1 onClickListener;

    @NotNull
    public final String getText() {
        return this.text;
    }

    public final void setText(@NotNull String var1) {
        Intrinsics.checkParameterIsNotNull(var1, "<set-?>");
        this.text = var1;
    }

    public final int getBackgroundColor() {
        return this.backgroundColor;
    }

    public final void setBackgroundColor(int var1) {
        this.backgroundColor = var1;
    }

    @Nullable
    public final Function1 getOnClickListener() {
        return this.onClickListener;
    }
```

```
    public final void setOnClickListener(@Nullable Function1 var1) {
        this.onClickListener = var1;
    }

    public Button() {
        throw (Throwable)(new NotImplementedError((String)null, 1,
(DefaultConstructorMarker)null));
    }
}
```

Under the hood, we have a usual class with getters and setters. The constructor throws an exception because we use the TODO() function.

Let's look at the Button class can be implemented in Java using *fields*:

```
public final class Button {
    @NotNull
    public String text;
    public int backgroundColor;
    @Nullable
    public Function1 onClickListener;
}
```

As you can see, in Kotlin, properties include **fields**, **getters**, and **setters**.

Let's define a custom getter and setter for the property:

```
var text: String = TODO()
    set(value) {
        println(value)
        field = value
    }
    get() {
        return field + field
    }
```

Now, decompiled to Java, the version code looks like this:

```
private String text;

@NotNull
public final String getText() {
    return this.text + this.text;
}

public final void setText(@NotNull String value) {
    Intrinsics.checkParameterIsNotNull(value, "value");
    System.out.println(value);
```

```
        this.text = value;
    }
```

In the preceding code snippet, getter and setter use the field identifier to access a backing field.

Backing fields

A **backing field** provides access to a field of a property. The setter method for the `text` property compiles to the following bytecode:

```
public final setText(Ljava/lang/String;)V
@Lorg/jetbrains/annotations/NotNull;() // invisible, parameter 0
L0
ALOAD 1
LDC "value"
INVOKESTATIC kotlin/jvm/internal/Intrinsics.checkParameterIsNotNull
(Ljava/lang/Object;Ljava/lang/String;)V
L1
LINENUMBER 89 L1
L2
GETSTATIC java/lang/System.out : Ljava/io/PrintStream;
ALOAD 1
INVOKEVIRTUAL java/io/PrintStream.println (Ljava/lang/Object;)V
L3
L4
LINENUMBER 90 L4
ALOAD 0
ALOAD 1
PUTFIELD Button.text : Ljava/lang/String;
L5
LINENUMBER 91 L5
RETURN
L6
LOCALVARIABLE this LButton; L0 L6 0
LOCALVARIABLE value Ljava/lang/String; L0 L6 1
MAXSTACK = 2
MAXLOCALS = 2
```

In the preceding bytecode, you can see the PUTFIELD instruction, which puts the value variable into the text field. So we need a backing field to access a field of a property.

To demonstrate this, let's rewrite the `Button` class as follows:

```
class Button {

    var text: String? = null
        set(value) {
            println(value)
            text = value
        }
        get() {
            return field + field
        }

    var backgroundColor: Int? = null

    var onClickListener: ((Button) -> Unit)? = null

}
```

Let's run this code:

```
fun main(args: Array<String>) {

    Button().text = "Button"
}
```

Here we have a recursive invocation of the setter. The output looks like this:

```
Button
Button
Button
Button
Button
Button
java.lang.StackOverflowError
at java.io.Writer.write(Writer.java:157)
at java.io.PrintStream.write(PrintStream.java:525)
at java.io.PrintStream.print(PrintStream.java:669)
at java.io.PrintStream.println(PrintStream.java:823)
at Button.setText(Main.kt:82)
at Button.setText(Main.kt:83)
at Button.setText(Main.kt:83)
at Button.setText(Main.kt:83)
at Button.setText(Main.kt:83)
```

The following bytecode shows that the `setText` method invokes itself:

```
// access flags 0x11
public final setText(Ljava/lang/String;)V
@Lorg/jetbrains/annotations/Nullable;() // invisible, parameter 0
L0
LINENUMBER 82 L0
L1
GETSTATIC java/lang/System.out : Ljava/io/PrintStream;
ALOAD 1
INVOKEVIRTUAL java/io/PrintStream.println (Ljava/lang/Object;)V
L2
L3
LINENUMBER 83 L3
ALOAD 0
ALOAD 1
INVOKEVIRTUAL Button.setText (Ljava/lang/String;)V
L4
LINENUMBER 84 L4
RETURN
L5
LOCALVARIABLE this LButton; L0 L5 0
LOCALVARIABLE value Ljava/lang/String; L0 L5 1
MAXSTACK = 2
MAXLOCALS = 2
```

Let's suppose that we need to do something like this:

```kotlin
class Button {

    var text: String? = null
        set(value) {
            println(value)
            field = value
        }
        get() {
            return field + field
        }

    var backgroundColor: Int? = null

    var onClickListener: ((Button) -> Unit)? = null

    fun printText() {
        println(text)
    }

}
```

In the preceding code snippet, the `printText` method writes the value of the `text` property to the console. Let's look at the bytecode generated:

```
// access flags 0x11
public final printText()V
L0
LINENUMBER 96 L0
ALOAD 0
INVOKEVIRTUAL Button.getText ()Ljava/lang/String;
ASTORE 1
L1
GETSTATIC java/lang/System.out : Ljava/io/PrintStream;
ALOAD 1
INVOKEVIRTUAL java/io/PrintStream.println (Ljava/lang/Object;)V
L2
L3
LINENUMBER 97 L3
RETURN
L4
LOCALVARIABLE this LButton; L0 L4 0
MAXSTACK = 2
MAXLOCALS = 2
```

Here, we can see that the `printText` method can't access a field of the `text` property directly. It's common practice to use getters and setters instead of accessing fields directly in C-family languages; that way, the compiler can inline the access and refer to a field directly. But in some cases, for instance, in Android development, it's a bad idea to use getters and setters inside a class:

- Android versions 4.4 and lower use the *Dalvik* virtual machine, which is based on the **just-in-time** (**JIT**) compilation. This means that each time an application runs, Dalvik compiles bytecode to machine code.
- Android versions 4.4 and higher use **Android Runtime** (**ART**), which is based on the **ahead-of-time** (**AOT**) compilation. This means that bytecode is compiled to machine code once during installation.
- Android version 4.4 is included in both ranges because it supports both of the virtual machines and users can choose between them.

According to the **Android performance tips** (`https://developer.android.com/training/articles/perf-tips.html`), direct access to a field is about three times faster than invoking a getter in ART and seven times faster than accessing a field in Dalvik.

To provide direct access to a field, you can use backing properties.

Backing properties

If you want to do something that doesn't fit the backing fields scheme (as in the case described earlier), you can use backing properties. Let's rewrite the `Button` class to use backing properties:

```
class Button {

    private var _text: String? = null
    var text: String
        set(value) {
            println(value)
            _text = value
        }
        get() {
            return _text + _text
        }

    var backgroundColor: Int? = null

    var onClickListener: ((Button) -> Unit)? = null

    fun printText() {
        println(_text)
    }

}
```

Here it is decompiled to Java code:

```
public final class Button {
    private String _text;
    @Nullable
    private Integer backgroundColor;
    @Nullable
    private Function1 onClickListener;

    @NotNull
    public final String getText() {
        return Intrinsics.stringPlus(this._text, this._text);
    }

    public final void setText(@NotNull String value) {
        Intrinsics.checkParameterIsNotNull(value, "value");
        System.out.println(value);
        this._text = value;
    }
```

```
@Nullable
public final Integer getBackgroundColor() {
    return this.backgroundColor;
}

public final void setBackgroundColor(@Nullable Integer var1) {
    this.backgroundColor = var1;
}

@Nullable
public final Function1 getOnClickListener() {
    return this.onClickListener;
}

public final void setOnClickListener(@Nullable Function1 var1) {
    this.onClickListener = var1;
}

public final void printText() {
    String var1 = this._text;
    System.out.println(var1);
}
}
```

In the preceding code snippet, you can see that the Button class has only the _text field and its getter and setter. The printText method refers directly to the _text field. To be sure of this, we can look at the following bytecode:

```
public final printText()V
L0
LINENUMBER 97 L0
ALOAD 0
GETFIELD Button._text : Ljava/lang/String;
ASTORE 1
L1
GETSTATIC java/lang/System.out : Ljava/io/PrintStream;
ALOAD 1
INVOKEVIRTUAL java/io/PrintStream.println (Ljava/lang/Object;)V
L2
L3
LINENUMBER 98 L3
RETURN
L4
LOCALVARIABLE this LButton; L0 L4 0
MAXSTACK = 2
MAXLOCALS = 2
```

Hence, backing properties allow you to have full access to a field as in Java.

It's important to use the `private` modifier with a backing property. Let's rewrite the `Button` class as follows:

```
class Button {

    var _text: String? = null
    var text: String
        set(value) {
            println(value)
            _text = value
        }
        get() {
            return _text + _text
        }

    var backgroundColor: Int? = null

    var onClickListener: ((Button) -> Unit)? = null

    fun printText() {
        println(_text)
    }
}
```

Now, the `Button` class looks like this when decompiled to Java:

```
public final class Button {
    @Nullable
    private String _text;
    @Nullable
    private Integer backgroundColor;
    @Nullable
    private Function1 onClickListener;

    @Nullable
    public final String get_text() {
        return this._text;
    }

    public final void set_text(@Nullable String var1) {
        this._text = var1;
    }

    @NotNull
    public final String getText() {
```

```
        return Intrinsics.stringPlus(this._text, this._text);
    }

    public final void setText(@NotNull String value) {
        Intrinsics.checkParameterIsNotNull(value, "value");
        System.out.println(value);
        this._text = value;
    }

    @Nullable
    public final Integer getBackgroundColor() {
        return this.backgroundColor;
    }

    public final void setBackgroundColor(@Nullable Integer var1) {
        this.backgroundColor = var1;
    }

    @Nullable
    public final Function1 getOnClickListener() {
        return this.onClickListener;
    }

    public final void setOnClickListener(@Nullable Function1 var1) {
        this.onClickListener = var1;
    }

    public final void printText() {
        String var1 = this._text;
        System.out.println(var1);
    }
}
```

In the preceding snippet, you can see that without the `private` modifier, the _text field
has a needless getter and setter.

@JvmField annotation

Let's look at the `Point` class from the `java.awt` package:

```
public class Point extends Point2D implements java.io.Serializable {
    public int x;

    public int y;

    private static final long serialVersionUID = -5276940640259749850L;
```

```java
public Point() {
    this(0, 0);
}

public Point(Point p) {
    this(p.x, p.y);
}

public Point(int x, int y) {
    this.x = x;
    this.y = y;
}

public double getX() {
    return x;
}

public double getY() {
    return y;
}

@Transient
public Point getLocation() {
    return new Point(x, y);
}

public void setLocation(Point p) {
    setLocation(p.x, p.y);
}

public void setLocation(int x, int y) {
    move(x, y);
}

public void setLocation(double x, double y) {
    this.x = (int) Math.floor(x+0.5);
    this.y = (int) Math.floor(y+0.5);
}

public void move(int x, int y) {
    this.x = x;
    this.y = y;
}

public void translate(int dx, int dy) {
    this.x += dx;
    this.y += dy;
}
```

```
public boolean equals(Object obj) {
    if (obj instanceof Point) {
        Point pt = (Point)obj;
        return (x == pt.x) && (y == pt.y);
    }
    return super.equals(obj);
}

public String toString() {
    return getClass().getName() + "[x=" + x + ",y=" + y + "]";
}
}
```

In this class, the x and y fields have the `public` modifier. This class overrides the `equals()` and `toString()` methods and has some methods that you can manipulate with fields. Also, we can access fields of an instance of this class directly:

```
Point().x = 3
```

Let's try to write something similar in Kotlin using data classes. Data classes is an extremely powerful feature that helps you avoid writing a lot of boilerplate code. Let's look at the following example:

```
data class Point(var x: Int, var y: Int)
```

This class, when decompiled to Java, looks like this:

```
public final class Point {
    private int x;
    private int y;

    public final int getX() {
        return this.x;
    }

    public final void setX(int var1) {
        this.x = var1;
    }

    public final int getY() {
        return this.y;
    }

    public final void setY(int var1) {
        this.y = var1;
    }
```

```
public Point(int x, int y) {
    this.x = x;
    this.y = y;
}

public final int component1() {
    return this.x;
}

public final int component2() {
    return this.y;
}

@NotNull
public final Point copy(int x, int y) {
    return new Point(x, y);
}

public String toString() {
    return "Point(x=" + this.x + ", y=" + this.y + ")";
}

public int hashCode() {
    return this.x * 31 + this.y;
}

public boolean equals(Object var1) {
    if (this != var1) {
        if (var1 instanceof Point) {
            Point var2 = (Point)var1;
            if (this.x == var2.x && this.y == var2.y) {
                return true;
            }
        }

        return false;
    } else {
        return true;
    }
}
}
```

We can see that it overrides the `equals()`, `hashCode()`, `toString()`, and `copy()` methods. This feature can save us a lot of time during development and keeps our code clean. But the x and y fields have the `private` modifier and the class has getters and setters for them. That's not exactly what we want. When we access x or y, we're actually calling getters and setters.

To work around this, we can use the @JvmField annotation. Let's rewrite the Point class as follows:

```
data class Point(@JvmField var x: Int, @JvmField var y: Int)
```

Now, it looks like this when decompiled to Java:

```java
public final class Point {
    @JvmField
    public int x;
    @JvmField
    public int y;

    public Point(int x, int y) {
        this.x = x;
        this.y = y;
    }

    public final int component1() {
        return this.x;
    }

    public final int component2() {
        return this.y;
    }

    @NotNull
    public final Point copy(int x, int y) {
        return new Point(x, y);
    }

    public String toString() {
        return "Point(x=" + this.x + ", y=" + this.y + ")";
    }

    public int hashCode() {
        return this.x * 31 + this.y;
    }

    public boolean equals(Object var1) {
        if (this != var1) {
            if (var1 instanceof Point) {
                Point var2 = (Point)var1;
                if (this.x == var2.x && this.y == var2.y) {
                    return true;
                }
            }
        }
```

```
            return false;
        } else {
            return true;
        }
    }
}
```

The x and y fields are marked with the `public` modifier and there are no longer getters and setters for them.

Now we can add some methods to manipulate fields:

```
data class Point(@JvmField var x: Int, @JvmField var y: Int) {
    fun translate(dx: Int, dy: Int) {
        this.x += dx
        this.y += dy
    }
}
```

Another interesting point regarding data classes is that overridden methods include only properties from the primary constructor. For example, we can take advantage of this to create temporary properties that don't have to be considered when comparing two instances:

```
data class Point(@JvmField var x: Int, @JvmField var y: Int) {
    var isTranslated = false
    fun translate(dx: Int, dy: Int) {
        this.x += dx
        this.y += dy
        this.isTranslated = true
    }
}
```

Now we can use the `isTranslated` property without affecting the `equals()` method:

```
public boolean equals(Object var1) {
    if (this != var1) {
        if (var1 instanceof Point) {
            Point var2 = (Point)var1;
            if (this.x == var2.x && this.y == var2.y) {
                return true;
            }
        }

        return false;
    } else {
```

```
        return true;
    }
}
```

Properties inspection

You're now familiar with the key considerations of using properties and fields in Kotlin. Next, we'll use the Kotlin bytecode inspector to get into the following topics:

- Compile-time constants
- Inner classes
- lateinit

Compile-time constants

Kotlin is a more object-oriented language than Java because Kotlin doesn't have primitive types, static fields, or static functions. But it's not a secret that these can improve performance. In this section and the next section, we'll look at examples that will help you understand some nuances of Kotlin related to primitive types, static fields, and static functions.

A compile-time constant is a read-only variable that's initialized during compilation. It has to meet the following requirements:

- It has to be declared as top-level or a member of an object
- It has to be initialized with a string value of a primitive type
- It can't have a getter or setter

Let's look at the following example:

```
const val compileTime: Int = 5

fun compileTimeFunction() = compileTime + compileTime
```

In the `Main.kt` file, we defined a top-level compile-time constant and function. This code compiles to the following bytecode:

```
public final class MainKt {

    // access flags 0x19
    public final static I compileTime = 5
```

```
// access flags 0x19
public final static compileTimeFunction()I
L0
LINENUMBER 79 L0
BIPUSH 10
IRETURN
L1
MAXSTACK = 1
MAXLOCALS = 0

}
```

Decompiled to Java, it looks like this:

```java
public final class MainKt {
   public static final int compileTime = 5;

   public static final int compileTimeFunction() {
      return 10;
   }
}
```

As you can see, each *.kt file with top-level members compiles to a class with the Kt suffix. The compiled MainKt class contains only our constant and function. There's no additional method, such as a constructor. That's why it's better to define only compile-time constants in one file as top-level members. To understand this better, let's add a variable to the Main.kt file:

```kotlin
val point = Point()

const val compileTime: Int = 5

fun compileTimeFunction() = compileTime + compileTime
```

Here's the compiled bytecode:

```
public final class MainKt {

    private final static Ljava/awt/Point; point
    @Lorg/jetbrains/annotations/NotNull;() // invisible

    public final static getPoint()Ljava/awt/Point;
    @Lorg/jetbrains/annotations/NotNull;() // invisible
    L0
    LINENUMBER 77 L0
    GETSTATIC MainKt.point : Ljava/awt/Point;
    ARETURN
```

```
L1
MAXSTACK = 1
MAXLOCALS = 0

public final static I compileTime = 5

public final static compileTimeFunction()I
L0
LINENUMBER 81 L0
BIPUSH 10
IRETURN
L1
MAXSTACK = 1
MAXLOCALS = 0

static <clinit>()V
L0
LINENUMBER 77 L0
NEW java/awt/Point
DUP
INVOKESPECIAL java/awt/Point.<init> ()V
PUTSTATIC MainKt.point : Ljava/awt/Point;
RETURN
MAXSTACK = 2
MAXLOCALS = 0
}
```

As you can see, the compiler generates a special <clinit> initializer method that initializes the point variable. Moreover, the point variable is marked with the private modifier, and to access it we have to use the getPoint() method. To mark the point variable with the public modifier and avoid generating the getPoint() method, we can just use the @JvmField annotation:

```
@JvmField
val point = Point()

const val compileTime: Int = 5

fun compileTimeFunction() = compileTime + compileTime
```

But we still have the <clinit> method:

```
public final class MainKt {
    public final static Ljava/awt/Point; point
    @Lkotlin/jvm/JvmField;() // invisible
    @Lorg/jetbrains/annotations/NotNull;() // invisible
    public final static I compileTime = 5
```

```
        public final static compileTimeFunction()I
       L0
       LINENUMBER 82 L0
       BIPUSH 10
       IRETURN
       L1
       MAXSTACK = 1
       MAXLOCALS = 0
       static <clinit>()V
       L0
       LINENUMBER 78 L0
       NEW java/awt/Point
       DUP
       INVOKESPECIAL java/awt/Point.<init> ()V
       PUTSTATIC MainKt.point : Ljava/awt/Point;
       RETURN
       MAXSTACK = 2
       MAXLOCALS = 0
   }
```

So it's best not to use non-compile time constants as top-level members if possible.

Inner classes

Inner classes are used rarely, but here is one good example of how to use them:

```
class Main {

    inner class Inner {

        fun printValue() {
            println(value)
        }
    }

    private var value = "Value"

}
```

Here's the decompiled version of this code:

```
public final class Main {
    private String value = "Value";

    // $FF: synthetic method
    public static final void access$setValue$p(Main $this, @NotNull String
```

```
var1) {
    $this.value = var1;
}

public final class Inner {
    public final void printValue() {
        String var1 = Main.this.value;
        System.out.println(var1);
    }
}
}
```

The compiler considers `Main` and `Inner` as two separate classes, and generates special functions to enable the `Inner` class to access private members of the `Main` class. In the bytecode, you can see that the `printValue()` method actually invokes the `access$getValue$p` static function of the `Main` class:

```
public final printValue()V
L0
LINENUMBER 84 L0
ALOAD 0
GETFIELD Main$Inner.this$0 : LMain;
INVOKESTATIC Main.access$getValue$p (LMain;)Ljava/lang/String;
ASTORE 1
L1
GETSTATIC java/lang/System.out : Ljava/io/PrintStream;
ALOAD 1
INVOKEVIRTUAL java/io/PrintStream.println (Ljava/lang/Object;)V
L2
L3
LINENUMBER 85 L3
RETURN
L4
LOCALVARIABLE this LMain$Inner; L0 L4 0
MAXSTACK = 2
MAXLOCALS = 2
```

In Java, it's enough to declare the `value` variable with package access. But Kotlin doesn't have package access members. Instead, we can just give public access to the `value` variable:

```
class Main {
    inner class Inner {
        fun printValue() {
            println(value)
        }
    }
```

```
        var value = "Value"
}
```

This isn't enough, however, because the compiler generates the `value` variable marked with the `private` modifier, and the `Inner` class uses getters and setters:

```
@NotNull
private String value = "Value";

@NotNull
public final String getValue() {
    return this.value;
}

public final void setValue(@NotNull String var1) {
    Intrinsics.checkParameterIsNotNull(var1, "<set-?>");
    this.value = var1;
}
```

In the bytecode, you can see that the `Inner` class invokes the `getValue()` method:

```
public final printValue()V
L0
LINENUMBER 84 L0
ALOAD 0
GETFIELD Main$Inner.this$0 : LMain;
INVOKEVIRTUAL Main.getValue ()Ljava/lang/String;
ASTORE 1
L1
GETSTATIC java/lang/System.out : Ljava/io/PrintStream;
ALOAD 1
INVOKEVIRTUAL java/io/PrintStream.println (Ljava/lang/Object;)V
L2
L3
LINENUMBER 85 L3
RETURN
L4
LOCALVARIABLE this LMain$Inner; L0 L4 0
MAXSTACK = 2
MAXLOCALS = 2
```

We also have to mark the `value` property with the `@JvmField` annotation. After this, the decompiled version will look like this:

```
public final class Main {

    @JvmField
```

```
@NotNull
public String value = "Value";

public final class Inner {
    public final void printValue() {
        String var1 = Main.this.value;
        System.out.println(var1);
    }
}
}
```

lateinit

Sometimes, we need to initialize properties after class initialization and don't want to create a nullable type, for instance, if we use dependency injection:

```
@Inject lateinit var coffee: Coffee
```

 Dependency injection is an implementation of inversion of control. It assumes that we should pass objects of another type to methods or constructors instead of creation instances inside a class of this object. The @Inject annotation is used to identify an injectable method, constructor, or field.

It's better to use a primary constructor here, so as to avoid creating an instance without initialized properties:

```
class CoffeeShop @Inject constructor(val coffee: Coffee) {
```

But in Android, a constructor for classes, such as Activity and Service, is invoked by the operating system itself. And we can't override a constructor.

We can improve the situation by using a setter for initialization:

```
private var coffee: Coffee? = null
    @Inject set(value) {
        field = value
    }
```

Using this approach, we can mark a property with the private modifier and use a nullable type.

Another example of a case when we need the `lateinit` keyword is with objects that contain the `onCreate()` method:

```
class Main {
    private lateinit var name: String
    fun onCreate() {
        name = "Jack"
    }
}
```

In the bytecode, you can see that this class is compiled into a normal Java field:

```
public final class Main {
    private Ljava/lang/String; name

    public final onCreate()V
    L0
    LINENUMBER 84 L0
    ALOAD 0
    LDC "Jack"
    PUTFIELD Main.name : Ljava/lang/String;
    L1
    LINENUMBER 85 L1
    RETURN
    L2
    LOCALVARIABLE this LMain; L0 L2 0
    MAXSTACK = 2
    MAXLOCALS = 1

    public <init>()V
    L0
    LINENUMBER 79 L0
    ALOAD 0
    INVOKESPECIAL java/lang/Object.<init> ()V
    RETURN
    L1
    LOCALVARIABLE this LMain; L0 L1 0
    MAXSTACK = 1
    MAXLOCALS = 1
}
```

There's no overhead here. Take a look at the `name` property:

```
fun onCreate() {
    name = "Jack"
```

```
    println(name)
}
```

The bytecode for the preceding `name` property looks like this:

```
public final onCreate()V
L0
LINENUMBER 84 L0
ALOAD 0
LDC "Jack"
PUTFIELD Main.name : Ljava/lang/String;
L1
LINENUMBER 86 L1
ALOAD 0
GETFIELD Main.name : Ljava/lang/String;
DUP
IFNONNULL L2
LDC "name"
INVOKESTATIC
kotlin/jvm/internal/Intrinsics.throwUninitializedPropertyAccessException
(Ljava/lang/String;)V
L2
ASTORE 1
L3
GETSTATIC java/lang/System.out : Ljava/io/PrintStream;
ALOAD 1
INVOKEVIRTUAL java/io/PrintStream.println (Ljava/lang/Object;)V
L4
L5
LINENUMBER 87 L5
RETURN
L6
LOCALVARIABLE this LMain; L0 L6 0
MAXSTACK = 2
MAXLOCALS = 2
```

Whenever you try to get a value from the `name` property, an additional check is invoked:

```
IFNONNULL L2
LDC "name"
INVOKESTATIC
kotlin/jvm/internal/Intrinsics.throwUninitializedPropertyAccessException
(Ljava/lang/String;)V
```

So if you're going to use a value from a property that's marked with the `lateinit` keyword, you should store the value in a local variable:

```
fun onCreate() {
    name = "Jack"
    val name = this.name
    println(name)
}
```

In this case, a check will be invoked only once:

```
public final onCreate()V
 L0
 LINENUMBER 90 L0
 ALOAD 0
 LDC "Jack"
 PUTFIELD Main.name : Ljava/lang/String;
 L1
 LINENUMBER 92 L1
 ALOAD 0
 GETFIELD Main.name : Ljava/lang/String;
 DUP
 IFNONNULL L2
 LDC "name"
 INVOKESTATIC
kotlin/jvm/internal/Intrinsics.throwUninitializedPropertyAccessException
(Ljava/lang/String;)V
 L2
 ASTORE 1
 L3
 LINENUMBER 93 L3
 L4
 GETSTATIC java/lang/System.out : Ljava/io/PrintStream;
 ALOAD 1
 INVOKEVIRTUAL java/io/PrintStream.println (Ljava/lang/Object;)V
 L5
 L6
 LINENUMBER 94 L6
 RETURN
 L7
 LOCALVARIABLE name Ljava/lang/String; L3 L7 1
 LOCALVARIABLE this LMain; L0 L7 0
 MAXSTACK = 2
 MAXLOCALS = 2
```

Or you can use some function, such as `also`:

```
fun onCreate() {
    name = "Jack"

    name.also {
        println(it)
    }
}
```

The `also` function is an inlined function, so the overhead is very low.

Companion objects

An object inside a class can be marked with the `companion` keyword. **Companion objects** are created when a class is loaded into memory. Working with members of companion objects is similar to working with static members, but you have to remember that these members are still instances of another class.

Let's look at the following example:

```
class Main private constructor() {

    private var id: Int? = null

    companion object {

        var prevId = -1

        fun newInstance(): Main {
            val main = Main()
            main.id = ++prevId
            return main
        }
    }
}
```

This code contains the `Main` class with a private constructor, the `id` property, and a companion object. The companion object has the `prevId` property. This property holds a unique identifier of a previously created instance of the `Main` class and the `newInstance()` method, which returns a new object of the `Main` class. The `newInstance()` method creates a new object, increments the value of the `prevId` property, and assigns it to the `id` property of the new object.

This simple code contains a lot of bottlenecks. Let's look at the bytecode. The `Main` class contains the `<clinit>` method, which is invoked during class loading and initializes a companion object:

```
static <clinit>()V
NEW Main$Companion
DUP
ACONST_NULL
INVOKESPECIAL Main$Companion.<init>
(Lkotlin/jvm/internal/DefaultConstructorMarker;)V
PUTSTATIC Main.Companion : LMain$Companion;
L0
LINENUMBER 94 L0
ICONST_M1
PUTSTATIC Main.id : I
RETURN
MAXSTACK = 3
MAXLOCALS = 0
```

Here we can see that the `<clinit>` method invokes a non-default constructor that's a special synthetic constructor for a companion object:

```
public synthetic <init>(Lkotlin/jvm/internal/DefaultConstructorMarker;)V
L0
LINENUMBER 92 L0
ALOAD 0
INVOKESPECIAL Main$Companion.<init> ()V
RETURN
L1
LOCALVARIABLE this LMain$Companion; L0 L1 0
LOCALVARIABLE $constructor_marker
Lkotlin/jvm/internal/DefaultConstructorMarker; L0 L1 1
MAXSTACK = 1
MAXLOCALS = 2
```

It is created alongside a default constructor:

```
private <init>()V
L0
LINENUMBER 94 L0
ALOAD 0
INVOKESPECIAL java/lang/Object.<init> ()V
RETURN
L1
LOCALVARIABLE this LMain$Companion; L0 L1 0
MAXSTACK = 1
MAXLOCALS = 1
```

The generated `Main$Companion` class also contains a getter and setter for the `prevId` variable:

```
public final getPrevId()I
L0
LINENUMBER 96 L0
INVOKESTATIC Main.access$getPrevId$cp ()I
IRETURN
L1
LOCALVARIABLE this LMain$Companion; L0 L1 0
MAXSTACK = 1
MAXLOCALS = 1

public final setPrevId(I)V
L0
LINENUMBER 96 L0
ILOAD 1
INVOKESTATIC Main.access$setPrevId$cp (I)V
RETURN
L1
LOCALVARIABLE this LMain$Companion; L0 L1 0
LOCALVARIABLE <set-?> I L0 L1 1
MAXSTACK = 1
MAXLOCALS = 2
```

These methods invoke other synthetic functions that provide access to the static `prevId` variable of the `Main` class:

```
public final static synthetic access$getPrevId$cp()I
   L0
    LINENUMBER 90 L0
    GETSTATIC Main.prevId : I
    IRETURN
   L1
    MAXSTACK = 1
    MAXLOCALS = 0

 // access flags 0x1019
 public final static synthetic access$setPrevId$cp(I)V
  L0
    LINENUMBER 90 L0
    ILOAD 0
    PUTSTATIC Main.prevId : I
    RETURN
   L1
```

```
    LOCALVARIABLE <set-?> I L0 L1 0
    MAXSTACK = 1
    MAXLOCALS = 1
```

The `Main` class also contains synthetic static functions that provide access to the `id` variable of the `Main` class:

```
public final static synthetic access$getId$p(LMain;)Ljava/lang/Integer;
@Lorg/jetbrains/annotations/Nullable;() // invisible
L0
LINENUMBER 90 L0
ALOAD 0
GETFIELD Main.id : Ljava/lang/Integer;
ARETURN
L1
LOCALVARIABLE $this LMain; L0 L1 0
MAXSTACK = 1
MAXLOCALS = 1

public final static synthetic access$setId$p(LMain;Ljava/lang/Integer;)V
@Lorg/jetbrains/annotations/Nullable;() // invisible, parameter 1
L0
LINENUMBER 90 L0
ALOAD 0
ALOAD 1
PUTFIELD Main.id : Ljava/lang/Integer;
RETURN
L1
LOCALVARIABLE $this LMain; L0 L1 0
LOCALVARIABLE <set-?> Ljava/lang/Integer; L0 L1 1
MAXSTACK = 2
MAXLOCALS = 2
```

As you can see, the `Main` class contains a lot of needless functions and methods. To work around this, we should rewrite the code as follows:

```
@file:JvmName("Main")

@JvmField
var prevId = -1

class Main private constructor() {

    private var id: Int? = null

    companion object {
```

```
        @JvmStatic
        fun newInstance(): Main {
            val main = Main()
            main.id = ++prevId
            return main
        }
    }
}
```

We already know how top-level members and the `@JvmField` annotation work. The `@file:JvmName("Main")` annotation tells the compiler that all top-level members have to be contained in the `Main` class. And the `@JvmStatic` annotation tells the compiler that the `newInstance()` function should be generated as static.

Now we have only one extra method:

```
public synthetic <init>(Lkotlin/jvm/internal/DefaultConstructorMarker;)V
L0
LINENUMBER 13 L0
ALOAD 0
INVOKESPECIAL com/fishduel/ruler/view/Main$Companion.<init> ()V
RETURN
L1
LOCALVARIABLE this Lcom/fishduel/ruler/view/Main$Companion; L0 L1 0
LOCALVARIABLE $constructor_marker
Lkotlin/jvm/internal/DefaultConstructorMarker; L0 L1 1
MAXSTACK = 1
MAXLOCALS = 2
```

Summary

In this chapter, we looked at the concept of properties in Kotlin, compared them to fields in Java, and learned how to avoid bottlenecks when using companion objects. We inspected a lot of examples in Kotlin, generated bytecode, and Kotlin code decompiled to Java.

In the next chapter, we'll learn how to prevent unnecessary overhead using the delegated pattern.

7
Preventing Unnecessary Overhead Using Delegates

Delegation is an extremely powerful pattern in which a delegating object assigns authority to a delegate object. The delegating object keeps a reference to the delegate object and dispatches messages to it.

 Dispatch, or message passing, is a concept in object-oriented programming by means of which one object invokes the method of another.

The delegating object uses the delegate object to provide an interface that's similar to an interface of the delegate. In some cases, the delegating object can send a message to the delegate object to just update its own state or that of another object. This is shown in the following diagram:

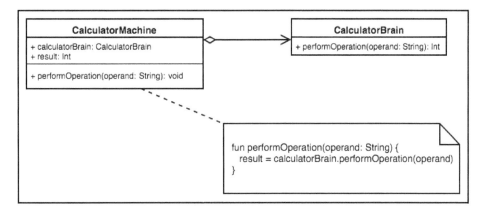

In other cases, the delegating object assigns responsibility for performing some behavior to the delegate object, as follows:

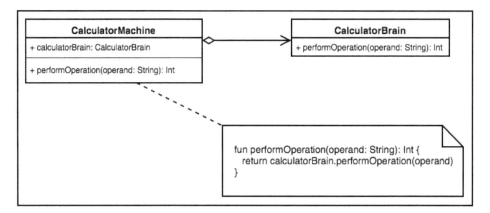

In this chapter, we'll cover the following topics:

- Types of delegation
- Class delegation
- Delegated properties

Types of delegation

There are two types of delegation:

- Explicit
- Implicit

Explicit delegation

Explicit delegation can be implemented by passing the delegate object to the delegating object. We can do this in any object-oriented language, such as Java. Let's create a `Calculator` interface:

```
public interface Calculator {
    int performOperation(String operand);
}
```

We'll also create a `CalculatorBrain` class that implements the `Calculator` interface:

```
public class CalculatorBrain implements Calculator {
    public int performOperation(String operand) {
        throw new IllegalStateException("Not implemented!");
    }
}
```

Now we'll implement a `CalculatorMachine` class. An instance of this class is a delegating object that delegates authority to an instance of `Calculator`, which is a delegate object. Let's create the `CalculatorMachine` class, which receives a `Calculator` instance using a constructor:

```
public class CalculatorMachine implements Calculator {

    private final Calculator delegate;

    public CalculatorMachine(Calculator delegate) {
        this.delegate = delegate;
    }
}
```

Since the `CalculatorMachine` class implements the `Calculator` interface, we have to implement the `performOperation()` method as follows:

```
@Override
public int performOperation(String operand) {
    return delegate.performOperation(operand);
}
```

The IntelliJ IDEA has a special function for this. Go to the `CalculatorMachine` class and open the **Generate** pane:

Then select a delegate object, as shown in the following screenshot:

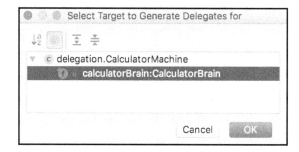

After which you select the methods as shown in the following screenshot:

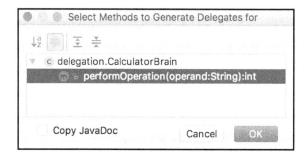

This function of IntelliJ IDEA is very useful if we have a lot of delegated methods.

We can pass an instance of any class that implements the `Calculator` interface. That's why delegation is an extremely powerful feature:

```
public class SuperCalculatorBrain implements Calculator {
    @Override
    public int performOperation(String operand) {
        throw new IllegalStateException("not implemented");
    }
}
```

The `main` function might look like this:

```
public static void main(String[] args) {
    new CalculatorMachine(new CalculatorBrain());
    new CalculatorMachine(new SuperCalculatorBrain());
}
```

We can even change a behavior of an instance of the `CalculatorMachine` class dynamically. All we need to do is make the `delegate` property non-final and create a setter:

```
public class CalculatorMachine implements Calculator {

    private Calculator delegate;

    public CalculatorMachine(Calculator delegate) {
        this.delegate = delegate;
    }

    public void setDelegate(Calculator delegate) {
        this.delegate = delegate;
    }

    @Override
    public int performOperation(String operand) {
        return delegate.performOperation(operand);
    }
}
```

Here's the `main` function:

```
public static void main(String[] args) {
    final CalculatorMachine calculatorMachine = new CalculatorMachine(new
CalculatorBrain());
    calculatorMachine.setDelegate(new SuperCalculatorBrain());
}
```

The following diagram represents a class structure:

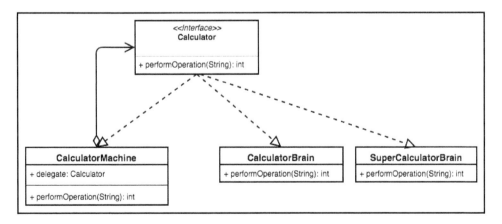

Implicit delegation

Implicit delegation is a language-level feature. With implicit delegation, we use a special language construction or keyword to implement delegation instead of overriding methods explicitly. There are two types of implicit delegation:

- Unanticipated
- Anticipated

For **unanticipated delegation**, a delegate object can be replaced by another dynamically, whereas **anticipated delegation** doesn't let us change a delegate object during the delegating object's life cycle.

Kotlin supports only anticipated delegation as a language-level feature, but if Kotlin-supported unanticipated delegation, it could look as follows:

```
class CalculatorMachine(var delegate: Calculator): Calculator by delegate
val calculator = CalculatorMachine(simpleCalculator)
calculator.delegate = superCalculator
```

The preceding code snippet shows that, using unanticipated delegation, we can change the delegate object after creating the delegating object.

Class delegation

Let's rewrite the `CalculatorMachine` class in Kotlin:

```
class CalculatorMachine(private val delegate: Calculator): Calculator by
delegate
```

That's it. Now you can use the `CalculatorMachine` class written in Kotlin similarly to the version written in Java:

```
fun main (args: Array<String>) {
    CalculatorMachine(CalculatorBrain())
}
```

You can see that the compiler generates the same bytecode for the Kotlin version of the `CalculatorMachine` class as for the Java version:

```
public final class delegation/kotlin/CalculatorMachine implements
delegation/Calculator  {
    private final Ldelegation/Calculator; delegate
    public <init>(Ldelegation/Calculator;)V
```

```
    @Lorg/jetbrains/annotations/NotNull;() // invisible, parameter 0
    L0
    ALOAD 1
    LDC "delegate"
    INVOKESTATIC kotlin/jvm/internal/Intrinsics.checkParameterIsNotNull
(Ljava/lang/Object;Ljava/lang/String;)V
    L1
    LINENUMBER 6 L1
    ALOAD 0
    INVOKESPECIAL java/lang/Object.<init> ()V
          ALOAD 0
    ALOAD 1
    PUTFIELD delegation/kotlin/CalculatorMachine.delegate :
Ldelegation/Calculator;
    RETURN
    L2
    LOCALVARIABLE this Ldelegation/kotlin/CalculatorMachine; L0 L2 0
    LOCALVARIABLE delegate Ldelegation/Calculator; L0 L2 1
    MAXSTACK = 2
    MAXLOCALS = 2
    public performOperation(Ljava/lang/String;)I
    L0
    ALOAD 0
    GETFIELD delegation/kotlin/CalculatorMachine.delegate :
Ldelegation/Calculator;
    ALOAD 1
    INVOKEINTERFACE delegation/Calculator.performOperation
(Ljava/lang/String;)I
    IRETURN
    L1
    LOCALVARIABLE this Ldelegation/kotlin/CalculatorMachine; L0 L1 0
    LOCALVARIABLE operand Ljava/lang/String; L0 L1 1
    MAXSTACK = 2
    MAXLOCALS = 2
}
```

The CalculatorMachine class, decompiled to Java, looks like this:

```
public final class CalculatorMachine implements Calculator {
   private final Calculator delegate;

   public CalculatorMachine(@NotNull Calculator delegate) {
      Intrinsics.checkParameterIsNotNull(delegate, "delegate");
      super();
      this.delegate = delegate;
   }

   public int performOperation(String operand) {
```

```
        return this.delegate.performOperation(operand);
    }
}
```

The class delegation feature of Kotlin uses the `by` keyword to specify a delegate object.

We can rewrite the `CalculatorMachine` class as follows:

```
class CalculatorMachine(var delegate: Calculator): Calculator by delegate
```

When decompiled to Java, it looks like this:

```
public final class CalculatorMachine implements Calculator {
    @NotNull
    private Calculator delegate;
    // $FF: synthetic field
    private final Calculator $$delegate_0;

    @NotNull
    public final Calculator getDelegate() {
        return this.delegate;
    }

    public final void setDelegate(@NotNull Calculator var1) {
        Intrinsics.checkParameterIsNotNull(var1, "<set-?>");
        this.delegate = var1;
    }

    public CalculatorMachine(@NotNull Calculator delegate) {
        Intrinsics.checkParameterIsNotNull(delegate, "delegate");
        super();
        this.$$delegate_0 = delegate;
        this.delegate = delegate;
    }

    public int performOperation(String operand) {
        return this.$$delegate_0.performOperation(operand);
    }
}
```

As you can see, a compiler generates the synthetic `$$delegate_0` field that has `private` and `final` modifiers. This field is used as a delegate object. The compiler also generates the `delegate` field with a getter and setter.

This example demonstrates that the class delegation feature implements the anticipated delegation pattern. And we can't replace a delegate object by another one dynamically. So there isn't any point in using the `var` modifier for a delegate object.

Let's imagine that we're going to create many instances of the `CalculatorMachine` class that use the same instance of the `CalculatorBrain` class. We can use the `object` keyword for `CalculatorBrain`:

```
object CalculatorBrain: Calculator {
    override fun performOperation(operand: String): Int = TODO()
}
```

And now we can rewrite the `CalculatorMachine` class as follows:

```
class CalculatorMachine(): Calculator by CalculatorBrain
```

Now, decompiled to Java, the `CalculatorMachine` class looks like this:

```
public final class CalculatorMachine implements Calculator {
    // $FF: synthetic field
    private final CalculatorBrain $$delegate_0;

    public CalculatorMachine() {
        this.$$delegate_0 = CalculatorBrain.INSTANCE;
    }

    public int performOperation(String operand) {
        return this.$$delegate_0.performOperation(operand);
    }
}
```

Now, we can create a new instance of the `CalculatorMachine` class without passing a delegate object:

```
fun main (args: Array<String>) {
    CalculatorMachine()
}
```

We don't have to create a new instance of the `CalculatorBrain` class all the time. This example demonstrates a good approach to implementing similar cases.

You can add additional methods that use a delegate object:

```
class CalculatorMachine(): Calculator by CalculatorBrain {

    fun printDelagateClassName() {
        println(CalculatorBrain::class.java.simpleName)
    }
}
```

Now, decompiled to Java, the `CalculatorMachine` class looks like this:

```java
public final class CalculatorMachine implements Calculator {
    // $FF: synthetic field
    private final CalculatorBrain $$delegate_0;

    public final void printDelagateClassName() {
        String var1 = delegation.CalculatorBrain.class.getSimpleName();
        System.out.println(var1);
    }

    public CalculatorMachine() {
        this.$$delegate_0 = CalculatorBrain.INSTANCE;
    }

    public int performOperation(String operand) {
        return this.$$delegate_0.performOperation(operand);
    }
}
```

If we rewrite `CalculatorBrain` back to the `CalculatorMachine` class, it looks as follows:

```kotlin
class CalculatorMachine(private val delegate: Calculator): Calculator by
delegate {
    fun printDelagateClassName() {
        println(delegate::class.java.simpleName)
    }
}
```

Now, the version that has been decompiled to Java looks the same as it did previously:

```java
public final class CalculatorMachine implements Calculator {
    private final Calculator delegate;

    public final void printDelagateClassName() {
        String var1 = this.delegate.getClass().getSimpleName();
        System.out.println(var1);
    }

    public CalculatorMachine(@NotNull Calculator delegate) {
        Intrinsics.checkParameterIsNotNull(delegate, "delegate");
        super();
        this.delegate = delegate;
    }

    public int performOperation(String operand) {
```

```
        return this.delegate.performOperation(operand);
    }
}
```

Class delegation is a good and more flexible alternative to implementation inheritance. Let's consider the next example. The Android SDK contains a fundamental class for Android development—`Activity`. A virtual machine invokes a default constructor and creates a new instance of this class by itself. So we can't override the constructor of our class that inherits from the `Activity` class. But we can use class delegation with a singleton in the form of a delegate object.

In our multiplatform project, we have a list of items. Let's create a click listener for items from this list.

The Android SDK contains the `OnClickListener` interface:

```
public interface OnClickListener {
    void onClick(View v);
}
```

Let's create a singleton that will implement this interface and show a message:

```
object OnItemClickListener : View.OnClickListener {
    override fun onClick(v: View?) {
        v?.also {
            Toast.makeText(it.context, (v as TextView).text,
Toast.LENGTH_LONG).show()
        }
    }
}
```

The `ItemsAdapter` class will receive this as an instance with the `OnClickListener` type as an argument:

```
class ItemsAdapter(private val onItemClickListener: View.OnClickListener)
```

It will set the `onItemClickListener` variable as a click listener for each item:

```
holder?.itemView?.setOnClickListener(onItemClickListener)
```

The `MainActivity` class will implement the `OnClickListener` interface and delegate authority for implementation to the `OnItemClickListener` object:

```
class MainActivity : AppCompatActivity(), View.OnClickListener by
OnItemClickListener
```

And we can just pass the `this` variable to a constructor of the `ItemsAdapter` class:

```
val adapter = ItemsAdapter(this)
```

Now, we can run our project and click on an item:

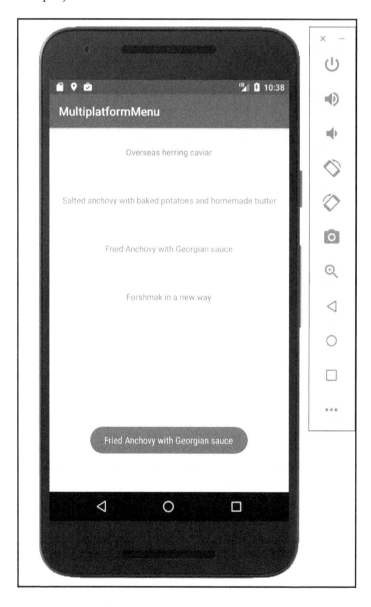

As you can see, class delegation is a good alternative to an inheritance, which can help you work around some common problems.

Delegated properties

Kotlin supports hybrid delegation in the form of delegated properties. Class delegation is based on the supertype. This means that both delegate and delegating classes implement the same interface. With class delegation, the delegate object is a parent of the delegating object.

The concept of hybrid delegation, on the other hand, doesn't require common implementation of a common interface or any parent-to-child relations. Instead, public methods of the delegate object take a reference to a delegating object as an argument. This allows the delegate object to use public methods of a delegating object.

The Kotlin standard library contains several useful implementations that use delegated properties.

Lazy

Let's consider the following example:

```
val lazyValue by lazy {
    BigInteger.valueOf(2).modPow(BigInteger.valueOf(7),
BigInteger.valueOf(20))
}
```

The `modPow` method of the `BigInteger` class performs modular exponentiation. It's an extremely useful function in public-key cryptography. This calculation can take some time, which is why we wrapped it up in the `Lazy<T>` delegate.

The `Lazy` delegate supports lazy evaluation. It's a common strategy that delays invoking an expression until its value is needed and caches the value to avoid repeated evaluations. Using this strategy can increase performance and avoid error conditions during computation.

The `Lazy` delegate supports three modes:

```
public enum class LazyThreadSafetyMode {
    SYNCHRONIZED,
    PUBLICATION,
    NONE,
}
```

Here is a short explanation of the different modes:

- The `SYNCHRONIZED` mode uses locks to ensure that only a single thread can evaluate a value.
- The `PUBLICATION` mode allows several threads to initialize a value, but only the first returned result will be used as the value.
- The `NONE` mode allows several threads to initialize a value, but its behavior is undefined.

The `Lazy.kt` file contains several overloaded versions of the `lazy` function. We used the first one in the preceding example:

```
public fun <T> lazy(initializer: () -> T): Lazy<T> =
SynchronizedLazyImpl(initializer)
```

This is a higher-order function that takes the `initializer` lambda and returns an instance of the `SynchronizedLazyImpl` class.

The `SynchronizedLazyImpl` class looks like this:

```
private class SynchronizedLazyImpl<out T>(initializer: () -> T, lock: Any?
= null) : Lazy<T>, Serializable {
    private var initializer: (() -> T)? = initializer
    @Volatile private var _value: Any? = UNINITIALIZED_VALUE
    // final field is required to enable safe publication of constructed
instance
    private val lock = lock ?: this

    override val value: T
        get() {
            val _v1 = _value
            if (_v1 !== UNINITIALIZED_VALUE) {
                @Suppress("UNCHECKED_CAST")
                return _v1 as T
            }

            return synchronized(lock) {
                val _v2 = _value
```

```
            if (_v2 !== UNINITIALIZED_VALUE) {
                @Suppress("UNCHECKED_CAST") (_v2 as T)
            }
            else {
                val typedValue = initializer!!()
                _value = typedValue
                initializer = null
                typedValue
            }
        }
    }

    override fun isInitialized(): Boolean = _value !== UNINITIALIZED_VALUE

    override fun toString(): String = if (isInitialized()) value.toString()
else "Lazy value not initialized yet."

    private fun writeReplace(): Any = InitializedLazyImpl(value)
}
```

As you can see, the getter for the `value` property uses the `synchronized` block to provide safe access in a concurrent environment.

This class implements the `Lazy` interface:

```
public interface Lazy<out T> {
    public val value: T
    public fun isInitialized(): Boolean
}
```

The second overloaded version of the `lazy` function looks like this:

```
public fun <T> lazy(mode: LazyThreadSafetyMode, initializer: () -> T):
Lazy<T> =
        when (mode) {
            LazyThreadSafetyMode.SYNCHRONIZED ->
SynchronizedLazyImpl(initializer)
            LazyThreadSafetyMode.PUBLICATION ->
SafePublicationLazyImpl(initializer)
            LazyThreadSafetyMode.NONE -> UnsafeLazyImpl(initializer)
        }
```

This function takes an instance of the `LazyThreadSafetyMode` enum so you can specify a mode explicitly.

You can use the NONE mode if your application works in a single-thread environment. For instance, in Android development, we can use it to initialize view instances:

```
private val rv by lazy(LazyThreadSafetyMode.NONE) {
    findViewById<RecyclerView>(R.id.rv)
}
```

Since the Android operating system works with instances of the Activity class using only one special UI thread, you can be sure that there isn't concurrent access to the instance of the Lazy class in this case.

The UnsafeLazyImpl class looks like this:

```
internal class UnsafeLazyImpl<out T>(initializer: () -> T) : Lazy<T>,
Serializable {
    private var initializer: (() -> T)? = initializer
    private var _value: Any? = UNINITIALIZED_VALUE

    override val value: T
        get() {
            if (_value === UNINITIALIZED_VALUE) {
                _value = initializer!!()
                initializer = null
            }
            @Suppress("UNCHECKED_CAST")
            return _value as T
        }

    override fun isInitialized(): Boolean = _value !== UNINITIALIZED_VALUE

    override fun toString(): String = if (isInitialized()) value.toString()
else "Lazy value not initialized yet."

    private fun writeReplace(): Any = InitializedLazyImpl(value)
}
```

As you can see, this class just checks whether the value is initialized and returns the cached value or evaluates a new one.

The following simplified example demonstrates a case when we can use the PUBLICATION mode. Let's suppose that we have two data sources. The first source loads data from a server and the second from the cache. They work on separate threads:

```
class CacheThread(val lazyValue: BigInteger): Thread() {
    override fun run() {
        super.run()
        Thread.sleep(250)
```

```
            println("${this::class.java.simpleName} $lazyValue")
        }
    }

    class NetworkThread(val lazyValue: BigInteger): Thread() {
        override fun run() {
            super.run()
            Thread.sleep(300)
            println("${this::class.java.simpleName} $lazyValue")
        }
    }
```

Loading data takes some time, and both threads need to evaluate the `lazyValue` variable in order to decrypt the received data.

The `main` method of our application looks like this:

```
val lazyValue by lazy(LazyThreadSafetyMode.PUBLICATION) {
    println("computation")
    BigInteger.valueOf(2).modPow(BigInteger.valueOf(7),
BigInteger.valueOf(20))
}

CacheThread(lazyValue).start()
NetworkThread(lazyValue).start()
```

The output will look as follows:

```
computation
CacheThread 8
NetworkThread 8
```

As you can see, the `initializer` lambda computes a value only once, when the `CacheThread` refers to the `lazyValue` variable, and then caches it. The `NetworkThread` retrieves a cached value instead of repeating computations.

The `SafePublicationLazyImpl` class looks like this:

```
private class SafePublicationLazyImpl<out T>(initializer: () -> T) :
Lazy<T>, Serializable {
    @Volatile private var initializer: (() -> T)? = initializer
    @Volatile private var _value: Any? = UNINITIALIZED_VALUE
    private val final: Any = UNINITIALIZED_VALUE

override val value: T
get() {
val value = _value
```

```
if (value !== UNINITIALIZED_VALUE) {
            @Suppress("UNCHECKED_CAST")
return value as T
        }

val initializerValue = initializer
        if (initializerValue != null) {
val newValue = initializerValue()
if (valueUpdater.compareAndSet(this, UNINITIALIZED_VALUE, newValue)) {
                initializer = null
                return newValue
        }
    }
        @Suppress("UNCHECKED_CAST")
return _value as T
    }

override fun isInitialized(): Boolean = _value !== UNINITIALIZED_VALUE

override fun toString(): String = if (isInitialized()) value.toString()
else "Lazy value not initialized yet."

    private fun writeReplace(): Any = InitializedLazyImpl(value)

companion object {
private val valueUpdater =
java.util.concurrent.atomic.AtomicReferenceFieldUpdater.newUpdater(
            SafePublicationLazyImpl::class.java,
            Any::class.java,
"_value")
    }
}
```

The `Lazy.kt` file contains the `getValue` extension function:

```
public inline operator fun <T> Lazy<T>.getValue(thisRef: Any?, property:
KProperty<*>): T = value
```

To understand what this function does, we need to know how to create a delegated property.

Creating a delegated property

For a read-only property marked with the `val` keyword, a delegated class has to have a `getValue()` method that takes the following arguments:

- `thisRef`: A reference to a delegating object
- `property`: An instance of the `KProperty` class

 An instance of the `KProperty` type can be used to retrieve metadata about a property.

The `getValue()` method also has to return an instance that has the same type or supertype as a delegating property. It can be an extension function, as in the case of the `Lazy` class.

For a property marked with the `var` keyword, a delegate class also has to have a `setValue()` method that takes the following arguments:

- `thisRef`: A reference to an outer class
- `property`: An instance of the `KProperty` type
- `value`: An instance that has the same type or supertype as a delegating property

The `setValue()` method has to return an instance of the `Unit` type and can also be an extension function. Both methods have to be marked with the `operator` keyword.

To simplify the creation of a delegated property, you can implement the `ReadOnlyProperty` or `ReadWriteProperty` interface:

```
interface ReadOnlyProperty<in R, out T> {
    operator fun getValue(thisRef: R, property: KProperty<*>): T
}

interface ReadWriteProperty<in R, T> {
    operator fun getValue(thisRef: R, property: KProperty<*>): T
    operator fun setValue(thisRef: R, property: KProperty<*>, value: T)
}
```

The implementation of the `ReadWriteProperty` interface can look like this:

```
class MyDelegate<T> : ReadWriteProperty<Any?, T?> {

    private var value: T? = null
```

```
    override fun getValue(thisRef: Any?, property: KProperty<*>): T? {
        return value
    }

    override fun setValue(thisRef: Any?, property: KProperty<*>, value: T?)
{
        this.value = value
    }
}
```

We can use the `MyDelegate` class as follows:

```
fun main(args: Array<String>) {
    val value by MyDelegate<String>()
    println(value)
}
```

Since Kotlin 1.1, we've been able to use delegated properties with local variables.

If you want to use your own delegate with a local variable, the first generic has to have a nullable type. The `MyDelegate` class looks like a normal class:

```
public final class MyDelegate implements ReadWriteProperty {
    private Object value;

    @Nullable
    public Object getValue(@Nullable Object thisRef, @NotNull KProperty
property) {
        Intrinsics.checkParameterIsNotNull(property, "property");
        return this.value;
    }

    public void setValue(@Nullable Object thisRef, @NotNull KProperty
property, @Nullable Object value) {
        Intrinsics.checkParameterIsNotNull(property, "property");
        this.value = value;
    }
}
```

A compiler generates
`Intrinsics.checkParameterIsNotNull(property, "property");`
to check whether we have a method that takes an argument of a non-nullable type.

The generated `MainKt` class looks like this:

```
public final class MainKt {
   // $FF: synthetic field
   static final KProperty[] $$delegatedProperties = new
KProperty[]{(KProperty)Reflection.property0(new
PropertyReference0Impl(Reflection.getOrCreateKotlinPackage(MainKt.class,
"production sources for module KotlinPerfomance"), "value", "<v#0>"))};

   public static final void main(@NotNull String[] args) {
      Intrinsics.checkParameterIsNotNull(args, "args");
      MyDelegate var10000 = new MyDelegate();
      KProperty var2 = $$delegatedProperties[0];
      MyDelegate value = var10000;
      Object var3 = value.getValue((Object)null, var2);
      System.out.println(var3);
   }
}
```

In the preceding snippet, you can see that `null` is passed as the first parameter to the `getValue` method. This is because we use the `MyDelegate` delegate for a local variable.

We can use the following `MyDelegate` delegate for a property of the `Main` class:

```
class Main {
    val property by MyDelegate<String>()
}
```

And the bytecode will look like this:

```
public final class Main {
   // $FF: synthetic field
   static final KProperty[] $$delegatedProperties = new
KProperty[]{(KProperty)Reflection.property1(new
PropertyReference1Impl(Reflection.getOrCreateKotlinClass(Main.class),
"property", "getProperty()Ljava/lang/String;"))};
   @Nullable
   private final MyDelegate property$delegate = new MyDelegate();

   @Nullable
   public final String getProperty() {
      return (String)this.property$delegate.getValue(this,
$$delegatedProperties[0]);
   }
}
```

In this case, the `this` reference is passed as the first parameter to the `getValue` method so we can use a non-nullable type if we use our own delegate only for properties of a class.

Let's add another property that uses the same delegate:

```
class Main {
    val property by MyDelegate<String>()
    val property2 by MyDelegate<String>()
}
```

Here's the version that has decompiled to Java:

```
public final class Main {
    // $FF: synthetic field
    static final KProperty[] $$delegatedProperties = new
KProperty[]{(KProperty)Reflection.property1(new
PropertyReference1Impl(Reflection.getOrCreateKotlinClass(Main.class),
"property", "getProperty()Ljava/lang/String;")),
(KProperty)Reflection.property1(new
PropertyReference1Impl(Reflection.getOrCreateKotlinClass(Main.class),
"another", "getAnother()Ljava/lang/String;"))};
    @Nullable
    private final MyDelegate property$delegate = new MyDelegate();
    @Nullable
    private final MyDelegate another$delegate = new MyDelegate();

    @Nullable
    public final String getProperty() {
        return (String)this.property$delegate.getValue(this,
$$delegatedProperties[0]);
    }

    @Nullable
    public final String getAnother() {
        return (String)this.another$delegate.getValue(this,
$$delegatedProperties[1]);
    }
}
```

As you can see, a new instance is created whenever you use the `MyDelegate` class as a delegate. So, if possible, you should create your own delegate as a singleton object. For instance, the `getValue` method of the following delegate takes the name of a property and returns it:

```
object SingletonDelegate : ReadOnlyProperty<Any?, String?> {
    override fun getValue(thisRef: Any?, property: KProperty<*>): String? {
        return property.name
```

```
        }
    }
```

We can use it as follows:

```
class Main {
    val property by SingletonDelegate
    val another by SingletonDelegate
}
```

Here's the `main` function:

```
fun main(args: Array<String>) {
    println(Main().property)
}
```

The output looks like this:

property

In the bytecode, you can see that a singleton object is used for both properties:

```
public final class Main {
// $FF: synthetic field
    static final KProperty[] $$delegatedProperties = new
KProperty[]{(KProperty)Reflection.property1(new
PropertyReference1Impl(Reflection.getOrCreateKotlinClass(Main.class),
"property", "getProperty()Ljava/lang/String;")),
(KProperty)Reflection.property1(new
PropertyReference1Impl(Reflection.getOrCreateKotlinClass(Main.class),
"another", "getAnother()Ljava/lang/String;"))};
    @Nullable
private final SingletonDelegate property$delegate;
    @Nullable
private final SingletonDelegate another$delegate;

    @Nullable
public final String getProperty() {
return this.property$delegate.getValue(this, $$delegatedProperties[0]);
    }

    @Nullable
public final String getAnother() {
return this.another$delegate.getValue(this, $$delegatedProperties[1]);
    }

public Main() {
this.property$delegate = SingletonDelegate.INSTANCE;
```

```
    this.another$delegate = SingletonDelegate.INSTANCE;
    }
}
```

The `MyDelegate` class uses a generic, meaning that we can use it for a property with any type. Let's look at the following example:

```
class GenericDelegate<T> : ReadOnlyProperty<Any?, T?> {
    override fun getValue(thisRef: Any?, property: KProperty<*>): T? {
        TODO()
    }
}
```

We can use this delegate as follows:

```
class Main {
    val property by GenericDelegate<Int>()
    val another by GenericDelegate<Float>()
}
```

Here, it is decompiled to Java:

```
public final class Main {
    // $FF: synthetic field
    static final KProperty[] $$delegatedProperties = new
KProperty[]{(KProperty)Reflection.property1(new
PropertyReference1Impl(Reflection.getOrCreateKotlinClass(Main.class),
"property", "getProperty()Ljava/lang/Integer;")),
(KProperty)Reflection.property1(new
PropertyReference1Impl(Reflection.getOrCreateKotlinClass(Main.class),
"another", "getAnother()Ljava/lang/Float;"))};
    @Nullable
    private final GenericDelegate property$delegate = new GenericDelegate();
    @Nullable
    private final GenericDelegate another$delegate = new GenericDelegate();

    @Nullable
    public final Integer getProperty() {
        return (Integer)this.property$delegate.getValue(this,
$$delegatedProperties[0]);
    }

    @Nullable
    public final Float getAnother() {
        return (Float)this.another$delegate.getValue(this,
$$delegatedProperties[1]);
    }
}
```

As you can see, unnecessary boxing and unboxing occur all the time. In this case, it's better to create a special delegate for each primitive type:

```
class IntDelegate : ReadOnlyProperty<Any?, Int?> {

    override fun getValue(thisRef: Any?, property: KProperty<*>): Int? {
        TODO()
    }
}
```

And you can use this delegate instead of the previous one:

```
class Main {
    val property by IntDelegate()
    val another by GenericDelegate<Float>()
}
```

Here's the version that has been decompiled to Java:

```
public final class Main {
   // $FF: synthetic field
   static final KProperty[] $$delegatedProperties = new
KProperty[]{(KProperty)Reflection.property1(new
PropertyReference1Impl(Reflection.getOrCreateKotlinClass(Main.class),
"property", "getProperty()Ljava/lang/Integer;")),
(KProperty)Reflection.property1(new
PropertyReference1Impl(Reflection.getOrCreateKotlinClass(Main.class),
"another", "getAnother()Ljava/lang/Float;"))};
   @Nullable
   private final IntDelegate property$delegate = new IntDelegate();
   @Nullable
   private final GenericDelegate another$delegate = new GenericDelegate();

   @Nullable
   public final Integer getProperty() {
      return this.property$delegate.getValue(this,
$$delegatedProperties[0]);
   }

   @Nullable
   public final Float getAnother() {
      return (Float)this.another$delegate.getValue(this,
$$delegatedProperties[1]);
   }
}
```

We saw a similar approach in Chapter 4, *Functional Approach*, in the *Capturing and non-capturing lambdas* section for the `Ref.java` class. This class contains a generic nested class for objects and special classes for each primitive type:

```
public static final class ObjectRef<T> implements Serializable {
    public T element;

    @Override
    public String toString() {
        return String.valueOf(element);
    }
}

public static final class ByteRef implements Serializable {
    public byte element;

    @Override
    public String toString() {
        return String.valueOf(element);
    }
}

public static final class ShortRef implements Serializable {
    public short element;

    @Override
    public String toString() {
        return String.valueOf(element);
    }
}
```

Inspecting the lazy function

Let's inspect the `lazy` delegate:

```
fun main (args: Array<String>) {
    val lazyValue by lazy { }
}
```

The `lazy` function isn't an inline function, so the bytecode contains a separate class for the `initializer` lambda. The simplified bytecode for this class looks like this:

```
final class delegation/kotlin/MainKt$main$lazyValue$2 extends
kotlin/jvm/internal/Lambda  implements kotlin/jvm/functions/Function0  {
```

```
    public synthetic bridge invoke()Ljava/lang/Object;

    public final invoke()V

    <init>()V

    public final static Ldelegation/kotlin/MainKt$main$lazyValue$2;
INSTANCE

    static <clinit>()V
    final static INNERCLASS delegation/kotlin/MainKt$main$lazyValue$2 null
null
}
```

The simplified bytecode of the `Main` class looks like this:

```
public final class delegation/kotlin/MainKt {
    final static synthetic [Lkotlin/reflect/KProperty;
$$delegatedProperties
    static <clinit>()V
    public final static main([Ljava/lang/String;)V

    final static INNERCLASS delegation/kotlin/MainKt$main$lazyValue$2 null
null
}
```

In the preceding snippet, we can see that the compiler generates a static array of instances of the `KProperties` class and initializes it inside the `<clinit>` function.

The bytecode of the `main` function looks like this:

```
public final static main([Ljava/lang/String;)V
@Lorg/jetbrains/annotations/NotNull;() // invisible, parameter 0
L0
ALOAD 0
LDC "args"
INVOKESTATIC kotlin/jvm/internal/Intrinsics.checkParameterIsNotNull
(Ljava/lang/Object;Ljava/lang/String;)V
L1
LINENUMBER 7 L1
GETSTATIC delegation/kotlin/MainKt$main$lazyValue$2.INSTANCE :
Ldelegation/kotlin/MainKt$main$lazyValue$2;
CHECKCAST kotlin/jvm/functions/Function0
INVOKESTATIC kotlin/LazyKt.lazy
(Lkotlin/jvm/functions/Function0;)Lkotlin/Lazy;
GETSTATIC delegation/kotlin/MainKt.$$delegatedProperties :
[Lkotlin/reflect/KProperty;
```

```
ICONST_0
AALOAD
ASTORE 2
ASTORE 1
L2
LINENUMBER 10 L2
RETURN
L3
LOCALVARIABLE lazyValue Lkotlin/Lazy; L2 L3 1
LOCALVARIABLE args [Ljava/lang/String; L0 L3 0
MAXSTACK = 3
MAXLOCALS = 3
```

In the preceding snippet, the INSTANCE object of the generated class for the lambda is passed to the `lazy` function.

So the simplified version of the preceding example looks like this:

```
private val lazyValue$delegate = SynchronizedLazyImpl()
var lazyValue: BigInteger
    get() = lazyValue$delegate.getValue(this, this::lazyValue)
```

Observable delegates

The observer pattern is a commonly-used pattern in any programming language. The Kotlin standard library contains a special delegate that implements this pattern:

```
var subject: String by Delegates.observable("init value") {
    property, old, new ->
    println("$old -> $new")
}
```

In this code snippet, we can see a subject variable that has an observer. The observer is a lambda that's passed as the second parameter to the `observable` function. The `observable` function looks like this:

```
public inline fun <T> observable(initialValue: T, crossinline onChange:
(property: KProperty<*>, oldValue: T, newValue: T) -> Unit):
    ReadWriteProperty<Any?, T> = object :
ObservableProperty<T>(initialValue) {
        override fun afterChange(property: KProperty<*>, oldValue: T,
newValue: T) = onChange(property, oldValue, newValue)
    }
```

As you can see, the `observable` function invokes the lambda after each change of value. The logic of invoking the `afterChange` method is implemented inside the `ObservableProperty` class:

```
public abstract class ObservableProperty<T>(initialValue: T) :
ReadWriteProperty<Any?, T> {
    private var value = initialValue

    protected open fun beforeChange(property: KProperty<*>, oldValue: T,
newValue: T): Boolean = true

    protected open fun afterChange (property: KProperty<*>, oldValue: T,
newValue: T): Unit {}

    public override fun getValue(thisRef: Any?, property: KProperty<*>): T
{
        return value
    }

    public override fun setValue(thisRef: Any?, property: KProperty<*>,
value: T) {
        val oldValue = this.value
        if (!beforeChange(property, oldValue, value)) {
            return
        }
        this.value = value
        afterChange(property, oldValue, value)
    }
}
```

The `Delegates.kt` file contains another interesting delegate—the `vetoable` function:

```
var maxLength: String by Delegates.vetoable("init value") {
    property, oldValue, newValue ->
    newValue.length > oldValue.length
}
```

The lambda that's passed as the second parameter to the `vetoable` function returns a Boolean. Depending on the Boolean value, the `newValue` variable will be assigned to `value`. The `vetoable` function looks like this:

```
public inline fun <T> vetoable(initialValue: T, crossinline onChange:
(property: KProperty<*>, oldValue: T, newValue: T) -> Boolean):
    ReadWriteProperty<Any?, T> = object :
ObservableProperty<T>(initialValue) {
        override fun beforeChange(property: KProperty<*>, oldValue: T,
newValue: T): Boolean = onChange(property, oldValue, newValue)
    }
```

This function also uses the `ObservableProperty` class. The main logic of the `vetoable` function is implemented inside the `setValue` method:

```
public override fun setValue(thisRef: Any?, property: KProperty<*>, value:
T) {
        val oldValue = this.value
        if (!beforeChange(property, oldValue, value)) {
            return
        }
        this.value = value
        afterChange(property, oldValue, value)
    }
```

Summary

In this chapter, we looked at the delegation pattern and its types. We used the class delegation feature as a good alternative to inheritance. We learned how to create a new delegated property and how delegates from the Kotlin standard library work under the hood. Kotlin supports the delegation pattern as a language-level feature that allows you to write simple and reliable code.

In the next chapter, we'll learn how to work with ranges and identify performance issues.

8
Ranges and Identifying Performance Issues

A range represents an interval or a set of real values. Each value in this set lies between two other values, which represent the start and the end of the range. Kotlin has classes that represent ranges and functions for its creation.

There are three common types of range:

- **A range of variables**: A set of values defined by start and end values (for instance, the range -3 to 3 includes -3, -2, -1, 0, 1, 2, and 3)
- **The range of an array**: A range that's bound by the first and last values of an array
- **The range of an iterator**: This means that the range can be iterated over each value

In this chapter, we will cover the following topics:

- Ranges in Kotlin
- Range benchmarking

Ranges in Kotlin

To create ranges of variables in Kotlin, you can use the `rangeTo` extension function or the `..` operator of Kotlin. We can create a range of any `Comparable` type.

Let's look at the following example:

```
fun main(args: Array<String>) {
    val int = args[0].toInt()
    if (int in 0..10) {
```

```
        println(int)
    }
}
```

In this example, we retrieve a value from the `args` array.

> The `args` array contains command-line arguments that can be used to pass parameters or specify a configuration when an application is launched.

To run a program with parameters in IntelliJ IDEA, click **Run** and choose **Edit Configurations...**:

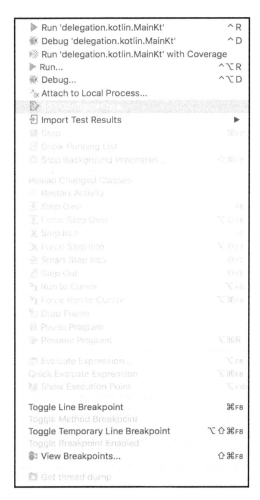

In the window that opens, you can paste parameters in the **Program arguments** field:

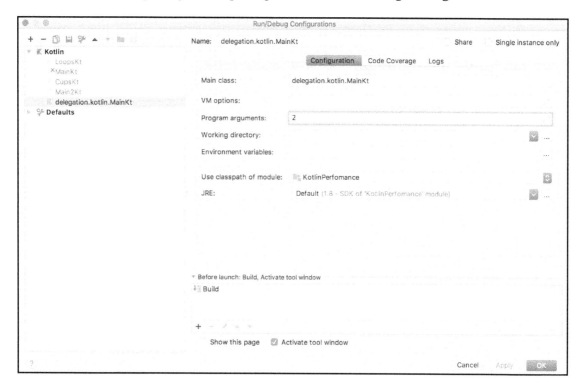

Press **OK** and run the application. The output will be as follows:

```
2
```

Decompiled to Java, it looks like the following:

```java
public static final void main(@NotNull String[] args) {
    Intrinsics.checkParameterIsNotNull(args, "args");
    String var2 = args[0];
    int value = Integer.parseInt(var2);
    if (0 <= value) {
        if (10 >= value) {
            System.out.println(value);
        }
    }
}
```

As you can see, there isn't any overhead here. We have a similar result with `double` and other primitive types:

```
fun main(args: Array<String>) {
    val value = args[0].toDouble()
    if (value in 0.0..10.0) {
        println(value)
    }
}
```

Here's the bytecode:

```
public static final void main(@NotNull String[] args) {
    Intrinsics.checkParameterIsNotNull(args, "args");
    String var3 = args[0];
    double value = Double.parseDouble(var3);
    if (value >= 0.0D && value <= 10.0D) {
        System.out.println(value);
    }
}
```

Let's suppose that the parameter is optional and that we have to use the `toIntOrNull()` method:

```
fun main(args: Array<String>) {
    val value = args[0].toIntOrNull()
    if (value in 0..10) {
        println(value)
    }
}
```

Here's the bytecode:

```
public static final void main(@NotNull String[] args) {
    Intrinsics.checkParameterIsNotNull(args, "args");
    Integer value = StringsKt.toIntOrNull(args[0]);
    byte var2 = 0;
    if (CollectionsKt.contains((Iterable)(new IntRange(var2, 10)), value)) {
        System.out.println(value);
    }
}
```

In this case, an instance of the `IntRange` class is created. The `Ranges.kt` file contains the CharRange, IntRange, and LongRange classes. The `IntRange` class looks like this:

```
public class IntRange(start: Int, endInclusive: Int) :
IntProgression(start, endInclusive, 1), ClosedRange<Int> {
    override val start: Int get() = first
    override val endInclusive: Int get() = last

    override fun contains(value: Int): Boolean = first <= value && value <=
last

    override fun isEmpty(): Boolean = first > last

    override fun equals(other: Any?): Boolean =
        other is IntRange && (isEmpty() && other.isEmpty() ||
        first == other.first && last == other.last)

    override fun hashCode(): Int =
        if (isEmpty()) -1 else (31 * first + last)

    override fun toString(): String = "$first..$last"

    companion object {
        /** An empty range of values of type Int. */
        public val EMPTY: IntRange = IntRange(1, 0)
    }
}
```

The CharRange and LongRange classes look similar to the `IntRange` class.
The `IntRange` class inherits from the `IntProgression` class, which looks like this:

```
public open class IntProgression internal constructor(start: Int,
endInclusive: Int, step: Int) : Iterable<Int> {
    init {
        if (step == 0) throw kotlin.IllegalArgumentException("Step must be
non-zero")
    }

    public val first: Int = start

    public val last: Int = getProgressionLastElement(start.toInt(),
endInclusive.toInt(), step).toInt()

    public val step: Int = step

    override fun iterator(): IntIterator = IntProgressionIterator(first,
last, step)
```

```
    public open fun isEmpty(): Boolean = if (step > 0) first > last else
first < last

    override fun equals(other: Any?): Boolean =
        other is IntProgression && (isEmpty() && other.isEmpty() ||
        first == other.first && last == other.last && step == other.step)

    override fun hashCode(): Int =
        if (isEmpty()) -1 else (31 * (31 * first + last) + step)

    override fun toString(): String = if (step > 0) "$first..$last step
$step" else "$first downTo $last step ${-step}"

    companion object {
        public fun fromClosedRange(rangeStart: Int, rangeEnd: Int, step:
Int): IntProgression = IntProgression(rangeStart, rangeEnd, step)
    }
}
```

This class is contained in the `Progressions.kt` file alongside the `LongPregression` and `CharProgression` classes.

The overridden `iterator()` method returns an instance of the `IntProgressionIterator` class. This class is contained in the `ProgressionIterates.kt` file alongside the `CharProgressionIterator` and `LongProgressionIterator` classes. The `IntProgressionIterator` class looks as follows:

```
internal class IntProgressionIterator(first: Int, last: Int, val step: Int)
: IntIterator() {
    private val finalElement = last
    private var hasNext: Boolean = if (step > 0) first <= last else first
>= last
    private var next = if (hasNext) first else finalElement

    override fun hasNext(): Boolean = hasNext

    override fun nextInt(): Int {
        val value = next
        if (value == finalElement) {
            if (!hasNext) throw kotlin.NoSuchElementException()
            hasNext = false
        }
        else {
            next += step
        }
```

```
        return value
    }
}
```

We use this class when we run code like this:

```
(0..10).forEach {

}
```

Here, it is decompiled to Java:

```
byte var1 = 0;
Iterable $receiver$iv = (Iterable)(new IntRange(var1, 10));

int element$iv;
for(Iterator var2 = $receiver$iv.iterator(); var2.hasNext(); element$iv =
((IntIterator)var2).nextInt()) {
    ;
}
```

The nextInt() method does the following:

- Retrieves the value stored in the next property
- Checks whether the value stored in the next property is equal to the value stored in the finalElement property
- If these values are equal, it assigns false to the hasNext property or adds the value of the step argument to the value of the next property and assigns the result to the next property
- Return the value variable

The IntRange class also implements the ClosedRange class, which looks like this:

```
public interface ClosedRange<T: Comparable<T>> {
    public val start: T

    public val endInclusive: T

    public operator fun contains(value: T): Boolean = value >= start &&
value <= endInclusive

    public fun isEmpty(): Boolean = start > endInclusive
}
```

The created `IntRange` is passed, along with the `value` variable, to the `contains` function of the `CollectionsKt` class.

The `contains` method looks like this:

```
public operator fun <@kotlin.internal.OnlyInputTypes T>
Iterable<T>.contains(element: T): Boolean {
    if (this is Collection)
        return contains(element)
    return indexOf(element) >= 0
}
```

Since a range isn't a collection, the `indexOf` method is invoked:

```
public fun <@kotlin.internal.OnlyInputTypes T> Iterable<T>.indexOf(element:
T): Int {
    if (this is List) return this.indexOf(element)
    var index = 0
    for (item in this) {
        if (element == item)
            return index
        index++
    }
    return -1
}
```

We have a similar case with a nullable character:

```
fun main(args: Array<String>) {
    val value: Char? = args[0].elementAtOrNull(0)
    if (value in 0.toChar()..10.toChar()) {
        println(value)
    }
}
```

And a nullable long:

```
fun main(args: Array<String>) {
    val value = args[0].toLongOrNull()
    if (value in 0L..10L) {
        println(value)
    }
}
```

We can also use nullable types of other primitives because they don't have classes similar to `IntRange`. There's a lot of overhead when we use ranges with nullable, so it's best not to.

We can use ranges with the `when` expression. The following example identifies the status of an HTTP response by its code:

```
val value = args[0].toInt()
when(value) {
    in 100..200 -> println("Informational responses")
    in 200..300 -> println("Success")
    in 300..400 -> println("Redirection")
    in 400..500 -> println("Client error")
    in 500..600 -> println("Server error")
}
```

This is what it looks like when decompiled to Java:

```
String var2 = args[0];
int value = Integer.parseInt(var2);
String var3;
if (100 <= value) {
    if (200 >= value) {
        var3 = "Informational responses";
        System.out.println(var3);
        return;
    }
}

if (200 <= value) {
    if (300 >= value) {
        var3 = "Success";
        System.out.println(var3);
        return;
    }
}

if (300 <= value) {
    if (400 >= value) {
        var3 = "Redirection";
        System.out.println(var3);
        return;
    }
}

if (400 <= value) {
    if (500 >= value) {
        var3 = "Client error";
```

```
            System.out.println(var3);
            return;
        }
    }

    if (500 <= value) {
        if (600 >= value) {
            var3 = "Server error";
            System.out.println(var3);
        }
    }
}
```

As you can see, it compiles in a usual sequence, so there isn't any overhead here.

But if the value variable has a nullable type:

```
val value = args[0].toIntOrNull()
```

Then it looks like this when decompiled to Java:

```
Integer value = StringsKt.toIntOrNull(args[0]);
byte var3 = 100;
String var4;
if (CollectionsKt.contains((Iterable)(new IntRange(var3, 200)), value)) {
    var4 = "Informational responses";
    System.out.println(var4);
} else {
    short var5 = 200;
    if (CollectionsKt.contains((Iterable)(new IntRange(var5, 300)), value))
{
        var4 = "Success";
        System.out.println(var4);
    } else {
        var5 = 300;
        if (CollectionsKt.contains((Iterable)(new IntRange(var5, 400)),
value)) {
            var4 = "Redirection";
            System.out.println(var4);
        } else {
            var5 = 400;
            if (CollectionsKt.contains((Iterable)(new IntRange(var5, 500)),
value)) {
                var4 = "Client error";
                System.out.println(var4);
            } else {
                var5 = 500;
                if (CollectionsKt.contains((Iterable)(new IntRange(var5, 600)),
value)) {
```

```
                var4 = "Server error";
                System.out.println(var4);
            }
        }
    }
}
```

We encounter a similar situation if we pass a `value` variable of the `Double` type to the `when` expression with ranges of the `Int` type:

```
val value = args[0].toDouble()
```

Here's the Java code for this:

```
String var3 = args[0];
double value = Double.parseDouble(var3);
byte var5 = 100;
String var6;
if (RangesKt.intRangeContains((ClosedRange)(new IntRange(var5, 200)),
value)) {
   var6 = "Informational responses";
   System.out.println(var6);
} else {
   short var7 = 200;
   if (RangesKt.intRangeContains((ClosedRange)(new IntRange(var7, 300)),
value)) {
      var6 = "Success";
      System.out.println(var6);
   } else {
      var7 = 300;
      if (RangesKt.intRangeContains((ClosedRange)(new IntRange(var7, 400)),
value)) {
         var6 = "Redirection";
         System.out.println(var6);
      } else {
         var7 = 400;
         if (RangesKt.intRangeContains((ClosedRange)(new IntRange(var7,
500)), value)) {
            var6 = "Client error";
            System.out.println(var6);
         } else {
            var7 = 500;
            if (RangesKt.intRangeContains((ClosedRange)(new IntRange(var7,
600)), value)) {
               var6 = "Server error";
               System.out.println(var6);
            }
```

```
                }
            }
        }
    }
```

We can avoid overhead if we use a `Double` variable with ranges of the `Double` type:

```
val value = args[0].toDouble()

when(value) {
    in 100.0..200.0 -> println("Informational responses")
    in 200.0..300.0 -> println("Success")
    in 300.0..400.0 -> println("Redirection")
    in 400.0..500.0 -> println("Client error")
    in 500.0..600.0 -> println("Server error")
}
```

Here's this same code decompiled to Java:

```
String var3 = args[0];
double value = Double.parseDouble(var3);
String var5;
if (value >= 100.0D && value <= 200.0D) {
    var5 = "Informational responses";
    System.out.println(var5);
} else if (value >= 200.0D && value <= 300.0D) {
    var5 = "Success";
    System.out.println(var5);
} else if (value >= 300.0D && value <= 400.0D) {
    var5 = "Redirection";
    System.out.println(var5);
} else if (value >= 400.0D && value <= 500.0D) {
    var5 = "Client error";
    System.out.println(var5);
} else if (value >= 500.0D && value <= 600.0D) {
    var5 = "Server error";
    System.out.println(var5);
}
```

Now, let's try passing a `value` variable of the `Long` type to the `when` expression, where the first three cases contain ranges of the `Long` type and the other two cases contain ranges of the `Double` type:

```
val value = args[0].toLong()
when(value) {
    in 100L..200L -> println("Informational responses")
    in 200L..300L -> println("Success")
```

```
    in 300L..400L -> println("Redirection")
    in 400.0..500.0 -> println("Client error")
    in 500.0..600.0 -> println("Server error")
}
```

Here's this code decompiled to Java:

```
String var3 = args[0];
long value = Long.parseLong(var3);
String var5;
if (100L <= value) {
    if (200L >= value) {
        var5 = "Informational responses";
        System.out.println(var5);
        return;
    }
}

if (200L <= value) {
    if (300L >= value) {
        var5 = "Success";
        System.out.println(var5);
        return;
    }
}

if (300L <= value) {
    if (400L >= value) {
        var5 = "Redirection";
        System.out.println(var5);
        return;
    }
}

if (RangesKt.doubleRangeContains((ClosedRange)RangesKt.rangeTo(400.0D,
500.0D), value)) {
    var5 = "Client error";
    System.out.println(var5);
} else if
(RangesKt.doubleRangeContains((ClosedRange)RangesKt.rangeTo(500.0D,
600.0D), value)) {
    var5 = "Server error";
    System.out.println(var5);
}
```

We should use ranges with variables of the same type and avoid nullable variables.

Utility functions

The _Ranges.kt file contains many utility functions for the IntProgression, LongProgression, and CharProgression classes. For instance, the reversed() function:

```
public fun IntProgression.reversed(): IntProgression {
    return IntProgression.fromClosedRange(last, first, -step)
}

public fun LongProgression.reversed(): LongProgression {
    return LongProgression.fromClosedRange(last, first, -step)
}

public fun CharProgression.reversed(): CharProgression {
    return CharProgression.fromClosedRange(last, first, -step)
}
```

One use of this function might look as follows:

```
fun main(args: Array<String>) {
    val value = args[0].toInt()
    if (value in (0..10).reversed()) {
        println(value)
    }
}
```

Decompiled to Java, it looks like this:

```
public final class MainKt {
    public static final void main(@NotNull String[] args) {
        Intrinsics.checkParameterIsNotNull(args, "args");
        String var2 = args[0];
        int value = Integer.parseInt(var2);
        byte var3 = 0;
        if
(CollectionsKt.contains((Iterable)RangesKt.reversed((IntProgression)(new
IntRange(var3, 10))), value)) {
            System.out.println(value);
        }
    }
}
```

The `fromClosedRange` function is a function of the `companion object` of the `IntProgression` class:

```
companion object {
    public fun fromClosedRange(rangeStart: Int, rangeEnd: Int, step: Int):
IntProgression = IntProgression(rangeStart, rangeEnd, step)
}
```

So whenever you use the `reversed()` function, an extra object is created.

The `step` function works in a similar manner to `reversed()`:

```
public infix fun IntProgression.step(step: Int): IntProgression {
    checkStepIsPositive(step > 0, step)
    return IntProgression.fromClosedRange(first, last, if (this.step > 0)
step else -step)
}
```

We can use the `step` function as an operator:

```
if (value in 0..10 step 3) {
    println(value)
}
```

Or as a usual function:

```
if (value in (0..10).step(3)) {
    println(value)
}
```

The `_Ranges.kt` file also contains the overloaded `downTo` extension functions for the `Int`, `Long`, `Byte`, `Short`, and `Char` classes:

```
public infix fun Int.downTo(to: Byte): IntProgression {
    return IntProgression.fromClosedRange(this, to.toInt(), -1)
}

public infix fun Long.downTo(to: Byte): LongProgression {
    return LongProgression.fromClosedRange(this, to.toLong(), -1L)
}

public infix fun Byte.downTo(to: Byte): IntProgression {
    return IntProgression.fromClosedRange(this.toInt(), to.toInt(), -1)
}

public infix fun Short.downTo(to: Byte): IntProgression {
    return IntProgression.fromClosedRange(this.toInt(), to.toInt(), -1)
```

```
    }

    public infix fun Char.downTo(to: Char): CharProgression {
        return CharProgression.fromClosedRange(this, to, -1)
    }
```

The `Primitives.kt` file contains such classes as `Byte`, `Short`, `Int`, and `Long`. Each class contains the extension functions as follows:

```
    public operator fun rangeTo(other: Byte): IntRange

    public operator fun rangeTo(other: Short): IntRange

    public operator fun rangeTo(other: Int): IntRange

    public operator fun rangeTo(other: Long): LongRange
```

If you don't create a reference to a range, then the compiler will optimize the bytecode:

```
    if (value in 0.rangeTo(10)) {
        println(value)
    }
```

Decompiled to Java, the code looks like this:

```
    public static final void main(@NotNull String[] args) {
        Intrinsics.checkParameterIsNotNull(args, "args");
        String var2 = args[0];
        int value = Integer.parseInt(var2);
        if (0 <= value) {
            if (10 >= value) {
                System.out.println(value);
            }
        }
    }
```

If you create a reference to a range:

```
    val range = 0..10

    if (value in range) {
        println(value)
    }
```

Then the unnecessary `IntRange` object will be created:

```
byte var3 = 0;
IntRange range = new IntRange(var3, 10);
if (range.contains(value)) {
    System.out.println(value);
}
```

Range benchmarking

Since the `IntRange` class inherits from the `IntProgression` class which, in turn, implements the `Iterable` interface, we can invoke the `forEach` function:

```
(0..10).forEach {

}
```

Decompiled to Java, the code looks like this:

```
public static final void main(@NotNull String[] args) {
    Intrinsics.checkParameterIsNotNull(args, "args");
    byte var1 = 0;
    Iterable $receiver$iv = (Iterable)(new IntRange(var1, 10));

    int element$iv;
    for(Iterator var2 = $receiver$iv.iterator(); var2.hasNext(); element$iv
= ((IntIterator)var2).nextInt()) {
        ;
    }
}
```

Let's write it and run some benchmarks:

```
val range = 0..1_000
val array = Array(1_000) { it }

@Benchmark
fun rangeLoop(blackhole: Blackhole) {
    range.forEach {
        blackhole.consume(it)
    }
}

@Benchmark
fun rangeSequenceLoop(blackhole: Blackhole) {
    range.asSequence().forEach {
```

```
        blackhole.consume(it)
    }
}

@Benchmark
fun arrayLoop(blackhole: Blackhole) {
    array.forEach {
        blackhole.consume(it)
    }
}

@Benchmark
fun arraySequenceLoop(blackhole: Blackhole) {
    array.asSequence().forEach {
        blackhole.consume(it)
    }
}
```

And here are the functions decompiled to Java:

```
@Benchmark
public final void rangeLoop(@NotNull Blackhole blackhole) {
    Intrinsics.checkParameterIsNotNull(blackhole, "blackhole");
    Iterable $receiver$iv = (Iterable)MyBenchmarkKt.getRange();
    Iterator var3 = $receiver$iv.iterator();

    while(var3.hasNext()) {
        int element$iv = ((IntIterator)var3).nextInt();
        blackhole.consume(element$iv);
    }

}

@Benchmark
public final void rangeSequenceLoop(@NotNull Blackhole blackhole) {
    Intrinsics.checkParameterIsNotNull(blackhole, "blackhole");
    Sequence $receiver$iv =
CollectionsKt.asSequence((Iterable)MyBenchmarkKt.getRange());
    Iterator var3 = $receiver$iv.iterator();

    while(var3.hasNext()) {
        Object element$iv = var3.next();
        int it = ((Number)element$iv).intValue();
        blackhole.consume(it);
    }

}
```

```
@Benchmark
public final void arrayLoop(@NotNull Blackhole blackhole) {
    Intrinsics.checkParameterIsNotNull(blackhole, "blackhole");
    Object[] $receiver$iv = (Object[])MyBenchmarkKt.getArray();
    int var3 = $receiver$iv.length;

    for(int var4 = 0; var4 < var3; ++var4) {
        Object element$iv = $receiver$iv[var4];
        int it = ((Number)element$iv).intValue();
        blackhole.consume(it);
    }

}

@Benchmark
public final void arraySequenceLoop(@NotNull Blackhole blackhole) {
    Intrinsics.checkParameterIsNotNull(blackhole, "blackhole");
    Sequence $receiver$iv =
ArraysKt.asSequence((Object[])MyBenchmarkKt.getArray());
    Iterator var3 = $receiver$iv.iterator();

    while(var3.hasNext()) {
        Object element$iv = var3.next();
        int it = ((Number)element$iv).intValue();
        blackhole.consume(it);
    }

}
```

Here's the output:

```
Benchmark                    Mode Cnt Score        Error    Units
arrayLoop                    avgt 200 2640.670 ±  8.357   ns/op
arraySequenceLoop.           avgt 200 2817.694 ± 44.780   ns/op
rangeLoop                    avgt 200 3156.754 ± 27.725   ns/op
rangeSequenceLoop            avgt 200 5286.066 ± 81.330   ns/op
```

The `arrayLoop` function uses a simple `for` loop under the hood. That's why this function is a little bit faster than the `rangeLoop` that uses an instance of the `Iterator`.

Let's write the following benchmarks:

```
@Benchmark
fun rangeLoop(blackhole: Blackhole)
        = range
            .map { it * 2 }
            .first { it % 2 == 0 }
```

```
@Benchmark
fun rangeSequenceLoop(blackhole: Blackhole)
        = range.asSequence()
            .map { it * 2 }
            .first { it % 2 == 0 }

@Benchmark
fun arrayLoop(blackhole: Blackhole)
    = array
            .map { it * 2 }
            .first { it % 2 == 0 }

@Benchmark
fun arraySequenceLoop(blackhole: Blackhole)
    = array.asSequence()
            .map { it * 2 }
            .first { it % 2 == 0 }
```

Our code of `range` functions looks like this when decompiled to Java:

```
@Benchmark
public final int rangeLoop(@NotNull Blackhole blackhole) {
    Intrinsics.checkParameterIsNotNull(blackhole, "blackhole");
    Iterable $receiver$iv = (Iterable)MyBenchmarkKt.getRange();
    Collection destination$iv$iv = (Collection)(new
ArrayList(CollectionsKt.collectionSizeOrDefault($receiver$iv, 10)));
    Iterator var5 = $receiver$iv.iterator();

    while(var5.hasNext()) {
        int item$iv$iv = ((IntIterator)var5).nextInt();
        Integer var12 = item$iv$iv * 2;
        destination$iv$iv.add(var12);
    }

    $receiver$iv = (Iterable)((List)destination$iv$iv);
    Iterator var3 = $receiver$iv.iterator();

    Object element$iv;
    int it;
    do {
        if (!var3.hasNext()) {
            throw (Throwable)(new NoSuchElementException("Collection contains
no element matching the predicate."));
        }

        element$iv = var3.next();
        it = ((Number)element$iv).intValue();
    } while(it % 2 != 0);
```

```
    return ((Number)element$iv).intValue();
}

@Benchmark
public final int rangeSequenceLoop(@NotNull Blackhole blackhole) {
    Intrinsics.checkParameterIsNotNull(blackhole, "blackhole");
    Sequence $receiver$iv =
SequencesKt.map(CollectionsKt.asSequence((Iterable)MyBenchmarkKt.getRange()
), (Function1)null.INSTANCE);
    Iterator var3 = $receiver$iv.iterator();

    Object element$iv;
    int it;
    do {
        if (!var3.hasNext()) {
            throw (Throwable)(new NoSuchElementException("Sequence contains no
element matching the predicate."));
        }

        element$iv = var3.next();
        it = ((Number)element$iv).intValue();
    } while(it % 2 != 0);

    return ((Number)element$iv).intValue();
}
```

And here are the array functions:

```
@Benchmark
public final int arrayLoop(@NotNull Blackhole blackhole) {
    Intrinsics.checkParameterIsNotNull(blackhole, "blackhole");
    Object[] $receiver$iv = (Object[])MyBenchmarkKt.getArray();
    Object[] $receiver$iv$iv = $receiver$iv;
    Collection destination$iv$iv = (Collection)(new
ArrayList($receiver$iv.length));
    int it = $receiver$iv.length;

    for(int var6 = 0; var6 < it; ++var6) {
        Object item$iv$iv = $receiver$iv$iv[var6];
        int it = ((Number)item$iv$iv).intValue();
        Integer var13 = it * 2;
        destination$iv$iv.add(var13);
    }

    Iterable $receiver$iv = (Iterable)((List)destination$iv$iv);
    Iterator var15 = $receiver$iv.iterator();

    Object element$iv;
```

```
    do {
        if (!var15.hasNext()) {
            throw (Throwable)(new NoSuchElementException("Collection contains
no element matching the predicate."));
        }

        element$iv = var15.next();
        it = ((Number)element$iv).intValue();
    } while(it % 2 != 0);

    return ((Number)element$iv).intValue();
}

@Benchmark
public final int arraySequenceLoop(@NotNull Blackhole blackhole) {
    Intrinsics.checkParameterIsNotNull(blackhole, "blackhole");
    Sequence $receiver$iv =
SequencesKt.map(ArraysKt.asSequence((Object[])MyBenchmarkKt.getArray()),
(Function1)null.INSTANCE);
    Iterator var3 = $receiver$iv.iterator();

    Object element$iv;
    int it;
    do {
        if (!var3.hasNext()) {
            throw (Throwable)(new NoSuchElementException("Sequence contains no
element matching the predicate."));
        }

        element$iv = var3.next();
        it = ((Number)element$iv).intValue();
    } while(it % 2 != 0);

    return ((Number)element$iv).intValue();
}
```

And here's the output:

Benchmark	Mode	Cnt	Score	Error	Units
arrayLoop	avgt	200	6490.003	± 124.134	ns/op
arraySequenceLoop	avgt	200	14.841	± 0.483	ns/op
rangeLoop	avgt.	200	8268.058	± 179.797	ns/op
rangeSequenceLoop	avgt	200	16.109	± 0.128	ns/op

Let's benchmark the last example from the previous section:

```
@State(Scope.Thread)
open class MyState {
  val value = 3;
}

@Benchmark
fun benchmark1(blackhole: Blackhole, state: MyState) {
    val range = 0..10

    if (state.value in range) {
        blackhole.consume(state.value)
    }

    if (state.value in range) {
        blackhole.consume(state.value)
    }
}

@Benchmark
fun benchmark2(blackhole: Blackhole, state: MyState) {

    if (state.value in 0..10) {
        blackhole.consume(state.value)
    }

    if (state.value in 0..10) {
        blackhole.consume(state.value)
    }
}
```

The Java version looks like this:

```
@Benchmark
public final void benchmark1(@NotNull Blackhole blackhole, @NotNull
MyBenchmark.MyState state) {
   Intrinsics.checkParameterIsNotNull(blackhole, "blackhole");
   Intrinsics.checkParameterIsNotNull(state, "state");
   byte var4 = 0;
   IntRange range = new IntRange(var4, 10);
   if (range.contains(state.getValue())) {
      blackhole.consume(state.getValue());
   }
   if (range.contains(state.getValue())) {
      blackhole.consume(state.getValue());
   }
}
```

```
@Benchmark
public final void benchmark2(@NotNull Blackhole blackhole, @NotNull
MyBenchmark.MyState state) {
    Intrinsics.checkParameterIsNotNull(blackhole, "blackhole");
    Intrinsics.checkParameterIsNotNull(state, "state");
    int var3 = state.getValue();
    if (0 <= var3) {
        if (10 >= var3) {
            blackhole.consume(state.getValue());
        }
    }

    var3 = state.getValue();
    if (0 <= var3) {
        if (10 >= var3) {
            blackhole.consume(state.getValue());
        }
    }
}
```

Here's the output:

```
Benchmark   Mode   Cnt   Score     Error   Units
benchmark1  avgt   200   4.828 ±   0.018   ns/op
benchmark2  avgt   200   4.833 ±   0.045   ns/op
```

The invocation times of the benchmark1 and benchmark2 functions are almost the same, but the benchmark1 function creates an instance of the IntRange class.

Summary

In this chapter, we looked at the concept of ranges in Kotlin and investigated the Kotlin standard library. We tried out common uses of ranges and inspected bytecode. We learned that we should be careful with types when we work with ranges and benchmarked some examples.

In the next chapter, we'll learn how to work in a multithreading environment.

Multithreading and Reactive Programming

9

Multithreading is a long-standing practice in software engineering. It's an extremely powerful approach that's used in almost all applications. We need separate threads to keep the user interface responsive when we invoke a long-term job like an input-output request. You should understand what multithreading is and what you can achieve with this technique.

In this chapter, we will cover the following topics:

- Concurrency and parallelism
- Reactive programming
- Coroutines

Concurrency and parallelism

Multithreading is based on the concepts of concurrency and parallelism. **Concurrency** refers to the ability of a task to be split into independent subtasks that can be executed out of order without affecting the final result:

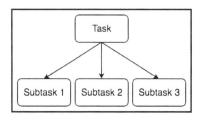

Let's look at the following example:

```
class Baker {
    fun bake(): Cake {
        for (i in 0..1_000_000_000) {
            BigInteger.ONE.modPow(BigInteger.TEN, BigInteger.TEN)
        }
        return Cake()
    }
}
```

The `Baker` class contains the `bake()` method, which invokes the `modPow` function that take a significant amount of time to imitate the process of baking and returns an instance of the `Cake` class:

```
class Cake
```

The `Bakery` class contains the `order` method, which takes the `numberOfCakes` argument and returns an instance of the `List<Cake>` type:

```
class Bakery {
    fun order(numberOfCakes: Int): List<Cake> {
        val cakes = mutableListOf<Cake>()
        val baker = Baker()
        val bakingTask = Runnable {
            cakes.add(baker.bake())
        }
        for (i in 0 until numberOfCakes) {
            bakingTask.run()
        }
        return cakes
    }
}
```

The `bakingTask` variable encapsulates a subtask. So whenever the `run()` method is invoked, a new subtask is started. The `main` function looks like this:

```
fun main(args: Array<String>) {
    val cakes = Bakery().order(amountOfCakes = 10)
    println("Number of cakes: ${cakes.size}")
}
```

The execution takes some time, and the output looks like this:

```
Number of cakes: 10
```

In the **Threads** pane, we can see that the program contains the `main` thread group with a single `main` thread:

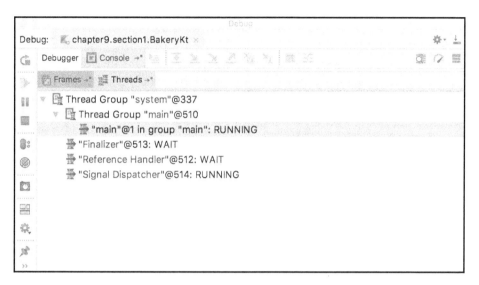

We know we have a concurrent program because it's split into subtasks. But these subtasks are executed sequentially, one after another:

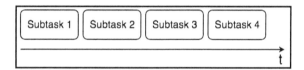

We can invoke each subtask in a separate thread:

```
fun fastOrder(amountOfCakes: Int): List<Cake> {
    val cakes = mutableListOf<Cake>()
    val baker = Baker()
    val bakingTask = Runnable {
        cakes.add(baker.bake())
    }
    val executor = Executors.newFixedThreadPool(amountOfCakes)
    for (i in 0 until amountOfCakes) {
        executor.execute(bakingTask)
    }
    executor.shutdown()
    return cakes
}
```

`Executors` is a class that contains factory methods to create new instances of the `ExecutorService` type. In fact, these methods create a pool of threads that can be reused, and `ExecutorService` is an interface that allows you to manage this pool. The `newFixedThreadPool(int nThreads)` method creates a pool that contains `nThreads` instances of the `Thread` class. The `execute(Runnable command)` method of the `Executor` interface executes the given instances of the `Runnable` interface at some time in the future. In our case, the given subtask will be invoked immediately if the pool contains a thread that isn't occupied with another subtask. Don't forget to call the `shutdown()` method to release the thread pool.

The **Threads** pane shows that the application has 10 additional threads that have the **RUNNING** status:

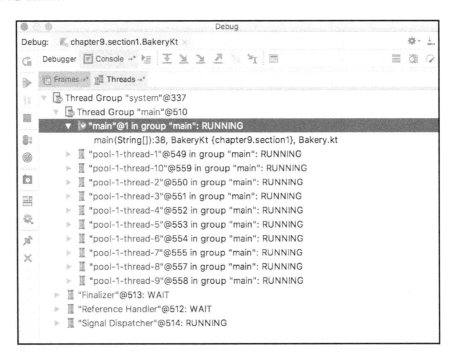

The output is printed immediately:

```
Number of cakes: 0
```

The number of cakes in the list is 0. This is because the `main` thread doesn't wait until other threads have completed subtasks.

To fix this, we can use the `CountDownLatch` class:

```
fun fastOrder(amountOfCakes: Int): List<Cake> {
    val cakes = mutableListOf<Cake>()
    val baker = Baker()
    val countDownLatch = CountDownLatch(amountOfCakes)
    val bakingTask = Runnable {
        cakes.add(baker.bake())
        countDownLatch.countDown()
    }
    val executor = Executors.newFixedThreadPool(amountOfCakes)
    for (i in 0 until amountOfCakes) {
        executor.execute(bakingTask)
    }
    executor.shutdown()
    countDownLatch.await()
    return cakes
}
```

The `CountDownLatch` class contains a counter and a thread, where the `await()` method is invoked until the counter isn't 0.

Here's the output:

Number of cakes: 10

Now, we can say that these 10 subtasks are executed pseudo-parallelly. We can split a task into subtasks programmatically, but the ability to execute these subtasks in parallel depends on hardware. To check our ability to do so, we can run the following code:

```
fun main(args: Array<String>) {
    val number = Runtime.getRuntime().availableProcessors()
    println("Number of available processors: $number")
}
```

On my computer, the output looks like this:

Number of available processors: 8

So, executing subtasks using the `fastOrder` method may look like this:

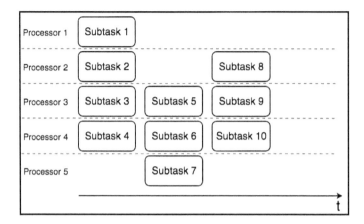

Parallelism refers to the ability to execute subtasks at the same time, and we need to have a sufficient number of free cores to execute subtasks that are truly in parallel.

Let's run the following benchmarks:

```
@BenchmarkMode(Mode.AverageTime)
@OutputTimeUnit(TimeUnit.SECONDS)
open class Benchmarks {

    @Benchmark
    fun order() = Bakery().order(amountOfCakes = 10)

    @Benchmark
    fun fastOrder() = Bakery().fastOrder(amountOfCakes = 10)

}
```

Here's the output:

```
Benchmark            Mode    Score    Units
Benchmarks.fastOrder avgt    9.884    s/op
Benchmarks.order     avgt    39.329   s/op
```

As you can see, the `fastOrder` method is four times faster than the `order` method. Therefore, we can significantly improve the performance of an application using multithreading. There are different approaches that can be used to deal with concurrency and one of them is reactive programming.

Reactive programming

Reactive programming is a style of programming that's focused on reacting to events. The most common implementation of reactive programming is the RxJava library. There's also an extension library for Kotlin called RxKotlin, which provides extension functions for RxJava that make programming more convenient.

We can use reactive programming to handle a sequence of events or a sequences of events. This approach is based on the observable pattern, and these are the two most frequently used interfaces in RxJava:

- ObservableSource: A basic interface for the Observable class:

```
public interface ObservableSource<T> {
    void subscribe(@NonNull Observer<? super T> var1);
}
```

- Observer: An interface that provides methods for receiving push-based notifications:

```
public interface Observer<T> {
    void onSubscribe(@NonNull Disposable var1);

    void onNext(@NonNull T var1);

    void onError(@NonNull Throwable var1);

    void onComplete();
}
```

Observable is a class that provides factory methods to create an instance of a certain implementation of the ObservableSource interface. The Observable class provides instances of the Observer type with the ability to consume synchronous and asynchronous data flows.

 With push-based notifications, an instance of the Observer type doesn't request data. Instead, an instance of the Observable class pushes a new event to the Observer using the onNext method.

Let's rewrite the bakery example using reactive programming.

The `Baker` class will contain the following method:

```
fun singleBake(): Single<Cake> {
    return Single.fromCallable {
        for (i in 0..1_000_000_000) {
            BigInteger.ONE.modPow(BigInteger.TEN, BigInteger.TEN)
        }
        Cake()
    }
}
```

The `Single` class works similarly to `Observable`, but it can emit only one event and terminates afterward. The `Single` class also has factory methods; `fromCallable`, which returns just a value method, is one of them. The `Single` class implements the `SingleSource` interface, which looks like this:

```
public interface SingleSource<T> {
    void subscribe(@NonNull SingleObserver<? super T> var1);
}
```

The `SingleSource` interface, similar to `ObservableSource`, contains one `subscribe` method that takes an instance of the `SingleObserver` interface. The `SingleObserver` interface looks as follows:

```
public interface SingleObserver<T> {
    void onSubscribe(@NonNull Disposable var1);

    void onSuccess(@NonNull T var1);

    void onError(@NonNull Throwable var1);
}
```

As you can see, it looks similar to the `Observer` interface but doesn't contain the `onComplete` and `onNext` methods. Instead, the `SingleObserver` interface contains the `onSuccess` method that's used to emit a value and notify a subscriber that an instance of the `Single` class has been terminated.

Let's add the `reactiveOrder` method to the `Bakery` class:

```
fun reactiveOrder(amountOfCakes: Int): Single<List<Cake>> {
    val baker = Baker()
    return Observable.range(0, amountOfCakes)
            .flatMapSingle { baker.singleBake() }
            .toList()
}
```

The range is a factory method of the Observable class. Let's look at the source code of the range method:

```
public static Observable<Integer> range(final int start, final int count) {
    if (count < 0) {
        throw new IllegalArgumentException("count >= 0 required but it was
" + count);
    }
    if (count == 0) {
        return empty();
    }
    if (count == 1) {
        return just(start);
    }
    if ((long)start + (count - 1) > Integer.MAX_VALUE) {
        throw new IllegalArgumentException("Integer overflow");
    }
    return RxJavaPlugins.onAssembly(new ObservableRange(start, count));
}
```

The range method takes two parameters, checks them, and returns the appropriate result. The ObservableRange class contains the nested RangeDisposable class, and the RangeDisposable class contains the run method, which contains the main logic of the range method:

```
void run() {
    if (fused) {
        return;
    }
    Observer<? super Integer> actual = this.actual;
    long e = end;
    for (long i = index; i != e && get() == 0; i++) {
        actual.onNext((int)i);
    }
    if (get() == 0) {
        lazySet(1);
        actual.onComplete();
    }
}
```

In short, the run method contains a simple loop that invokes the onNext method during each iteration. After this, the onComplete method is invoked to notify a subscriber that an Observable class has been terminated.

If the value of the `count` parameter is 0, the `range` function invokes the `empty` function:

```
public static <T> Observable<T> empty() {
    return RxJavaPlugins.onAssembly((Observable<T>)
ObservableEmpty.INSTANCE);
}
```

The `empty` function returns a singleton instance of the `ObservableEmpty` class:

```
public final class ObservableEmpty extends Observable<Object> implements
ScalarCallable<Object> {
    public static final Observable<Object> INSTANCE = new
ObservableEmpty();
    private ObservableEmpty() {}
    @Override
    protected void subscribeActual(Observer<? super Object> o) {
        EmptyDisposable.complete(o);
    }
    @Override
    public Object call() {
        return null; // null scalar is interpreted as being empty
    }
}
```

If the value of the `count` parameter is 0, the `range` function invokes the `just` function:

```
public static <T> Observable<T> just(T item) {
    ObjectHelper.requireNonNull(item, "The item is null");
    return RxJavaPlugins.onAssembly(new ObservableJust<T>(item));
}
```

The `just` function is useful when we want to create a new observable from a single value. The `ObservableJust` class looks as follows:

```
public final class ObservableJust<T> extends Observable<T> implements
ScalarCallable<T> {
    private final T value;
    public ObservableJust(final T value) {
        this.value = value;
    }
    @Override
    protected void subscribeActual(Observer<? super T> s) {
        ScalarDisposable<T> sd = new ScalarDisposable<T>(s, value);
        s.onSubscribe(sd);
        sd.run();
    }
    @Override
    public T call() {
```

```
            return value;
        }
    }
```

The `Observable` class contains a set of `flatMap*` family methods:

```
public final <R> Observable<R> flatMap(Function<? super T, ? extends
ObservableSource<? extends R>> mapper) {
    return flatMap(mapper, false);
}
```

The `flatMapSingle` method that takes an instance of `SingleSource` looks as follows:

```
public final <R> Observable<R> flatMapSingle(Function<? super T, ? extends
SingleSource<? extends R>> mapper) {
    return flatMapSingle(mapper, false);
}
```

The `flatMapMaybe` method that takes an instance of `MaybeSource` looks as follows:

```
public final <R> Observable<R> flatMapMaybe(Function<? super T, ? extends
MaybeSource<? extends R>> mapper, boolean delayErrors) {
    ObjectHelper.requireNonNull(mapper, "mapper is null");
    return RxJavaPlugins.onAssembly(new ObservableFlatMapMaybe<T, R>(this,
mapper, delayErrors));
}
```

The `flatMapIterable` method that takes an instance of `Iterable` looks as follows:

```
public final <U, V> Observable<V> flatMapIterable(final Function<? super T,
? extends Iterable<? extends U>> mapper,
        BiFunction<? super T, ? super U, ? extends V> resultSelector) {
    ObjectHelper.requireNonNull(mapper, "mapper is null");
    ObjectHelper.requireNonNull(resultSelector, "resultSelector is null");
    return flatMap(ObservableInternalHelper.flatMapIntoIterable(mapper),
resultSelector, false, bufferSize(), bufferSize());
}
```

The `flatMapCompletable` method that takes an instance of `CompletableSource` looks as follows:

```
public final Completable flatMapCompletable(Function<? super T, ? extends
CompletableSource> mapper, boolean delayErrors) {
    ObjectHelper.requireNonNull(mapper, "mapper is null");
    return RxJavaPlugins.onAssembly(new
ObservableFlatMapCompletableCompletable<T>(this, mapper, delayErrors));
}
```

The `flatMap` method allows you to map each value from an upstream of a dataflow to an instance of the `Single`, `Completable`, `Iterable`, `Maybe`, or `Observable` class. The `flatMap` method merges all results into a single observable and passes it to a downstream of the dataflow.

`Maybe` is a class that's similar to `Single`, but the `MaybeObserver` interface contains the `onComplete` method:

```
public interface MaybeObserver<T> {

    void onSubscribe(@NonNull Disposable d);

    void onSuccess(@NonNull T t);

    void onError(@NonNull Throwable e);

    void onComplete();
}
```

An instance of the `Maybe` class can emit a value using the `onSuccess` method or can just invoke the `onComplete` method without producing any value.

An instance of the `Completable` type doesn't emit any value but notifies an instance of the `CompletableObserver` class that some operation has completed. The `CompletableObserver` interface looks as follows:

```
public interface CompletableObserver {
    void onSubscribe(@NonNull Disposable d);

    void onComplete();

    void onError(@NonNull Throwable e);
}
```

Now, we can use the `reactiveOrder` method as follows:

```
Bakery().reactiveOrder(10)
        .subscribe { cakes ->  println("Number of cakes: ${cakes.size}")}
```

Here's the output:

```
Number of cakes: 10
```

This is an example of a synchronous instance of the `Single` class that works using one thread:

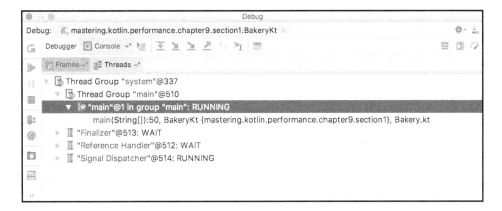

By synchronous, we mean that all actions are executed sequentially, one by one:

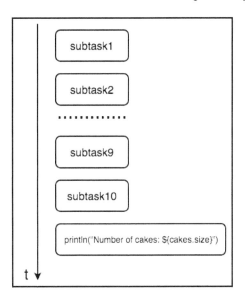

To run all subtasks in parallel, we can use the `subscribeOn` method:

```
fun singleBake(): Single<Cake> {
    return Single.fromCallable { bake()
}.subscribeOn(Schedulers.computation())
}
```

The `subscribeOn` method takes an instance of the `Scheduler` class. In short, the `Scheduler` class represents a pool of threads that can be used by an instance of the `Single` class.

The `Schedulers` class contains factory methods that return different instances of the `Scheduler` class that can be used for different purposes:

```
public final class Schedulers {
    ......
    public static Scheduler computation() {
        return RxJavaPlugins.onComputationScheduler(COMPUTATION);
    }
    public static Scheduler io() {
        return RxJavaPlugins.onIoScheduler(IO);
    }
    public static Scheduler trampoline() {
        return TRAMPOLINE;
    }
    public static Scheduler newThread() {
        return RxJavaPlugins.onNewThreadScheduler(NEW_THREAD);
    }
    public static Scheduler single() {
        return RxJavaPlugins.onSingleScheduler(SINGLE);
    }
    .......
}
```

The **Debugger** now shows additional threads:

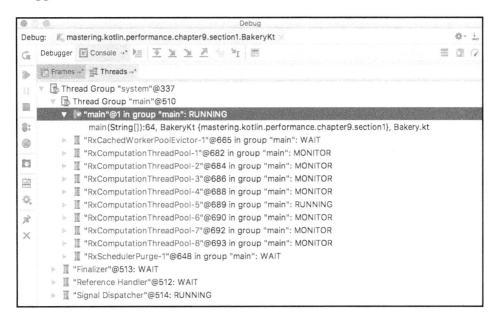

But the output is empty. This is because all of the threads run asynchronously and the program finished alongside the `main` thread:

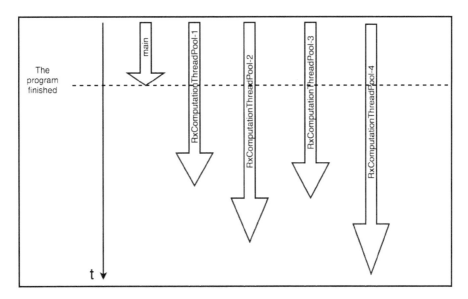

To fix this, we can use the `wait` and `notify` methods of the `java.lang.Object` class:

```
class Lock {

    private val lock = java.lang.Object()

    fun unlock() {
        synchronized(lock) {
            lock.notify()
        }
    }

    fun lock() {
        synchronized(lock) {
            lock.wait()
        }
    }
}
```

All classes in Kotlin inherit from `Any`, which doesn't contain the `notify`, `notifyAll`, and `wait` methods, but we can access the `Object` class by package name. The `Lock` class encapsulates the logic that we need to synchronize the work of the threads. The `unlock` method creates a synchronized block and invokes the `notify` method of the `lock` property. The `lock` method does the same but with the `wait` method. We need a synchronized block because the `wait` and `notify` methods throw `java.lang.IllegalMonitorStateException`.

We can use the `Lock` class as follows:

```
val lock = Lock()

Bakery().reactiveOrder(10)
        .doAfterTerminate { lock.unlock() }
        .subscribe { cakes ->  println("Number of cakes: ${cakes.size}")}

lock.lock()
```

The `doAfterTerminate` method is invoked when an instance of `Single` is terminated. We can use this to detect the moment when all threads have finished.

Using the **Debugger**, we can see that the `main` thread waits until all threads from the pool have finished:

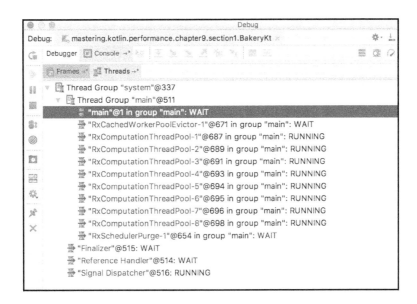

The following diagram shows the synchronized work of threads:

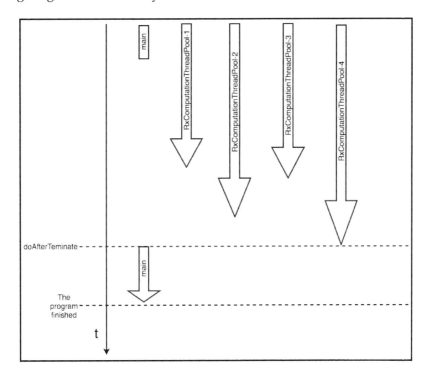

```
Number of cakes: 10
```

We can also use the `blocking*` family methods. We can use them as follows:

```
val cakes = Bakery().reactiveOrder(10).blockingGet()
println("Number of cakes: ${cakes.size}")
```

This method creates an instance of the `BlockingMultiObserver` class:

```
public final T blockingGet() {
    BlockingMultiObserver<T> observer = new BlockingMultiObserver<T>();
    subscribe(observer);
    return observer.blockingGet();
}
```

The `BlockingMultiObserver` class extends `CountDownLatch`:

```
public final class BlockingMultiObserver<T>
extends CountDownLatch
implements SingleObserver<T>, CompletableObserver, MaybeObserver<T> {
```

The `blockingGet` method of the `BlockingMultiObserver` class invokes the `await` method:

```
public T blockingGet() {
if (getCount() != 0) {
try {
            BlockingHelper.verifyNonBlocking();
            await();
        } catch (InterruptedException ex) {
            dispose();
throw ExceptionHelper.wrapOrThrow(ex);
        }
    }
    Throwable ex = error;
if (ex != null) {
throw ExceptionHelper.wrapOrThrow(ex);
    }
return value;
}
```

And terminating these methods invokes the `countDown` method:

```
@Override
public void onSuccess(T value) {
this.value = value;
```

```
        countDown();
    }

    @Override
    public void onError(Throwable e) {
    error = e;
        countDown();
    }

    @Override
    public void onComplete() {
        countDown();
    }
```

We can also use the `blockingGet` method to move from a declarative to an imperative style of programming.

The `Observable` class contains the `blockingSubscribe` method, which can be used as follows:

```
Bakery().reactiveOrder(10)
        .toObservable()
        .blockingSubscribe { cakes -> println("Number of cakes:
${cakes.size}")   }
```

This method is a good alternative to the `blockingGet` method. This section shows how to deal with multithreaded environment using reactive programming. We've learned that reactive programming is a good approach that allows you to write simple and reliable code to handle synchronous and asynchronous events. `RxJava` is an extremely powerful implementation of this style that contains a large code base with functions that can be useful for different cases.

Coroutines

Coroutines are an experimental feature of Kotlin that allow you to write asynchronous code sequentially. Their experimental nature means that this feature is still under development but that we can use it in production. The concept of coroutines is based on suspended computations that don't block a thread.

Coroutines in Kotlin are based on three things:

- Language-level support (the `suspend` keyword)
- Low-level core API from the Kotlin standard library
- High-level API

Setting up a project

If you use the Maven build system, you should add the following line to the `configuration` tag:

```
<arg>-Xcoroutines=enable</arg>
```

We need this because the coroutines feature has an experimental status now. The configuration tag will look as follows:

```
<configuration>
    <args>
        <arg>-Xcoroutines=enable</arg>
    </args>
</configuration>
```

To add the `kotlin-coroutines-core` library (`https://github.com/Kotlin/kotlinx.coroutines/tree/master/core/kotlinx-coroutines-core`), you should add the following dependency:

```
<dependency>
    <groupId>org.jetbrains.kotlinx</groupId>
    <artifactId>kotlinx-coroutines-core</artifactId>
    <version>0.21</version>
</dependency>
```

This library contains common functions, such as `launch` and `async`.

The launch function

The `launch` function can be used as follows:

```
val job = launch {
    val suspendLambda = suspend {
        delay(1, TimeUnit.SECONDS)
        println("Hello from suspend lambda")
    }
```

```
    suspendLambda()
}
```

The `suspend` modifier is used to specify that invoking of function can be suspended and can be called only from a coroutine. The `delay` function is a special function that can be used for examples or debugging. This function just pauses a coroutine on time that is passed as a parameter.

The `launch` function is a special function that can invoke `suspend` lambdas and functions:

```
public actual fun launch(
    context: CoroutineContext = DefaultDispatcher,
    start: CoroutineStart = CoroutineStart.DEFAULT,
    parent: Job? = null,
    block: suspend CoroutineScope.() -> Unit
): Job {
    val newContext = newCoroutineContext(context, parent)
    val coroutine = if (start.isLazy)
        LazyStandaloneCoroutine(newContext, block) else
        StandaloneCoroutine(newContext, active = true)
    coroutine.initParentJob(newContext[Job])
    start(block, coroutine, coroutine)
    return coroutine
}
```

This function returns an instance of the `Job` type. The simplified version of the `Job` class looks as follows:

```
public actual interface Job : CoroutineContext.Element {
    public actual val isActive: Boolean
    public actual val isCompleted: Boolean
    public actual val isCancelled: Boolean
    public actual fun start(): Boolean
    public actual fun cancel(cause: Throwable? = null): Boolean
    public actual suspend fun join()
}
```

The `Job` class represents a cancellable task that has a life cycle and can have children. During the life cycle, an instance of the `Job` type moves through the following states:

- New
- Active
- Completing

- Completed
- Canceling
- Canceled

The following diagram shows how a job moves through these states:

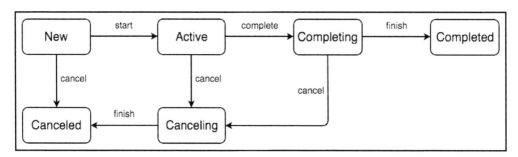

The `join` method of the `Job` class suspends a coroutine until the `Job` is done. This method is marked with the `suspend` keyword:

```
public actual suspend fun join()
```

We can invoke the `join` method from a function that has an instance of the `CoroutineContext`, for example, `launch`.

The `suspendLambda` function is invoked on a separate thread. Therefore, we need to force the `main` thread to wait until `suspendLambda` has finished. For this, we can use the `runBlocking` function:

```
fun main(args: Array<String>) = runBlocking {
    val job = launch {
        val suspendLambda = suspend {
            delay(1, TimeUnit.SECONDS)
            println("Hello from suspend lambda")
        }
        suspendLambda()
    }
    job.join()
}
```

The `runBlocking` function can call `suspend` lambdas or functions and block a thread where it's invoked:

```
public fun <T> runBlocking(context: CoroutineContext =
EmptyCoroutineContext, block: suspend CoroutineScope.() -> T): T {
    val currentThread = Thread.currentThread()
    val eventLoop = if (context[ContinuationInterceptor] == null)
BlockingEventLoop(currentThread) else null
    val newContext = newCoroutineContext(context + (eventLoop ?:
EmptyCoroutineContext))
    val coroutine = BlockingCoroutine<T>(newContext, currentThread,
privateEventLoop = eventLoop != null)
    coroutine.initParentJob(newContext[Job])
    block.startCoroutine(coroutine, coroutine)
    return coroutine.joinBlocking()
}
```

The async function

The `async` function creates a new coroutine and returns an instance of the `Deferred` type:

```
public actual fun <T> async(
    context: CoroutineContext = DefaultDispatcher,
    start: CoroutineStart = CoroutineStart.DEFAULT,
    parent: Job? = null,
    block: suspend CoroutineScope.() -> T
): Deferred<T> {
    val newContext = newCoroutineContext(context, parent)
    val coroutine = if (start.isLazy)
        LazyDeferredCoroutine(newContext, block) else
        DeferredCoroutine<T>(newContext, active = true)
    coroutine.initParentJob(newContext[Job])
    start(block, coroutine, coroutine)
    return coroutine
}
```

`Deferred` is an interface that represents a future result of a coroutine execution:

```
public actual interface Deferred<out T> : Job {
    public actual val isCompletedExceptionally: Boolean

    public actual suspend fun await(): T

    public val onAwait: SelectClause1<T>

    public actual fun getCompleted(): T
```

```
    public actual fun getCompletionExceptionOrNull(): Throwable?

    @Deprecated(message = "Use `isActive`", replaceWith =
ReplaceWith("isActive"))
    public val isComputing: Boolean get() = isActive
}
```

We can use the `async` function in the following way:

```
val deferredList = (0 until numberOfCakes).map { async { baker.bake() } }
```

This line of code does the following things:

- Creates a range from 0 to a value that's stored in the `numberOfCakes` variable
- Transforms each value in the range to an instance of the `Deferred` type

Inside the lambda that we pass to the `map` method, the `async` function is invoked. The `async` function, in turn, takes another lambda that invokes the `bake` method, which returns an instance of the `Cake` class. The `deferredList` variable contains a list of instances of the `Deferred<Cake>` type. Now, we can just invoke the `await` method of each deferred value in the list:

```
deferredList.forEach { cakes.add(it.await()) }
```

We can write all of this code in the chain style:

```
(0 until amountOfCakes)
        .map { async { baker.bake() } }
        .forEach { cakes.add(it.await()) }
```

The `coroutinesOrder` function looks like this:

```
suspend fun coroutinesOrder(amountOfCakes: Int): List<Cake> {
    val baker = Baker()
    return (0 until amountOfCakes)
            .map { async { baker.bake() } }
            .map { it.await()}
}
```

We can run this function using the following code:

```
fun main(args: Array<String>) = runBlocking {
    val cakes = Bakery().coroutinesOrder(10)
    println("Number of cakes: ${cakes.size}")
}
```

Here's the output:

Number of cakes: 10

The debugger shows that seven threads from `ForkJoinPool` are working in parallel:

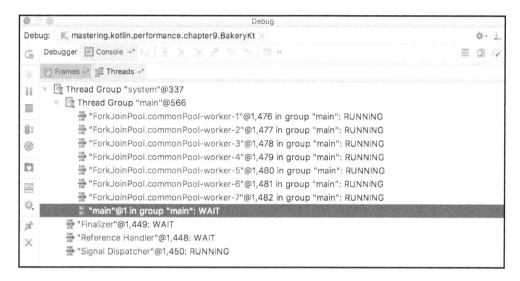

`ForkJoinPool` is a pool that contains a number of threads corresponding to the number of cores, minus one. The current implementation of the `coroutinesOrder` method looks good. Let's try other approaches.

The buildSequence function

We can try using the `buildSequence` function, which looks like this:

```
public fun <T> buildSequence(builderAction: suspend SequenceBuilder<T>.()
-> Unit): Sequence<T> = Sequence { buildIterator(builderAction) }
```

The `buildIterator` function looks as follows:

```
public fun <T> buildIterator(builderAction: suspend SequenceBuilder<T>.()
-> Unit): Iterator<T> {
    val iterator = SequenceBuilderIterator<T>()
    iterator.nextStep = builderAction.createCoroutineUnchecked(receiver =
iterator, completion = iterator)
    return iterator
```

The `buildSequence` function just returns an instance of the `Iterator` type and can be used as follows:

```
fun coroutinesSequenceOrder(amountOfCakes: Int) = buildSequence {
    val baker = Baker()
    (0 until amountOfCakes)
            .forEach { yield(baker.bake()) }
}.toList()
```

To run this function, we can use code like this:

```
fun main(args: Array<String>) = runBlocking {
    val cakes = Bakery().coroutinesSequenceOrder(10)
    println("Number of cakes: ${cakes.size}")
}
```

This approach looks better, but the debugger shows that we didn't launch new coroutines and our code uses only the `main` thread:

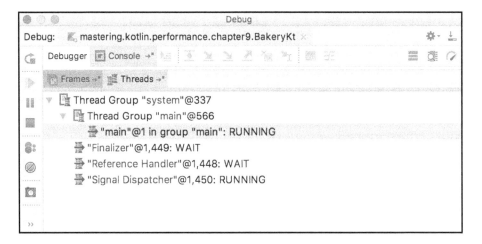

The suspendingSequence function

We can create our own `suspendingSequence` function using an example from GitHub (`https://github.com/Kotlin/kotlin-coroutines/blob/master/examples/suspendingSequence/suspendingSequence.kt`). This function creates a sequence that can run suspending functions and lambdas.

The `suspendingSequence` function can be used as follows:

```
suspend fun coroutinesSuspendingSequenceOrder(amountOfCakes: Int) =
suspendingSequence {
    (0 until amountOfCakes)
            .map { async { Baker().bake() } }
            .forEach { yield(it.await()) }
}.iterator().toList()
```

In the preceding snippet, the `coroutineSuspendingSequenceOrder` function contains a range from `0` to `amountOfCakes`. We map each value from the range to an instance of the `Deferred` class using the `async` function. We pass a lambda to the `async` function that invokes the `bake()` method. So the type of values that the `map` function returns is `Deferred<Cake>`. Then we use the `forEach` function to invoke the `await` method on each instance that was returned from `map`. The `await` function suspends, waits, and resumes the `main` thread until a new instance of the `Cake` class is ready. Then we use the `yield` function to pass created cake to a sequence. The **Debugger** shows that seven threads from `ForkJoinPool` run in parallel:

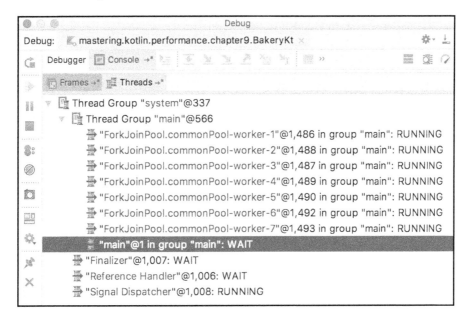

The produce function

The `produce` function is an implementation of the **producer-consumer** pattern. The responsibility of a producer is to send messages to a queue. A consumer, in turn, consumes these messages:

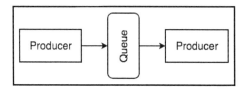

Our new `coroutinesProducerOrder` function looks like this:

```
suspend fun coroutinesProducerOrder(amountOfCakes: Int) = produce<Cake> {
    (0 until amountOfCakes)
            .map { async { Baker().bake() } }
            .forEach { send(it.await()) }
}.toList()
```

We can run this function using the following code:

```
fun main(args: Array<String>) = runBlocking {
    val cakes = Bakery().coroutinesProducerOrder(10)
    println("Number of cakes: ${cakes.size}")
}
```

Coroutines with reactive programming

You can easily combine your code written in a reactive style with coroutines. For this, you can use the `kotlinx-coroutines-rx2` module (`https://github.com/Kotlin/kotlinx.coroutines/tree/master/reactive/kotlinx-coroutines-rx2`).

This library contains a set of functions to convert coroutines to live collections from `RxJava`, such as `rxMaybe`, `rxCompletable`, `rxSingle`, `rxObservable`, and `rxFlowable`.

Or you can, for instance, invoke an `await*` family method of a live collection from `RxJava`. We can use this with our `reactiveOrder` method:

```
suspend fun rxToCoroutinesOrder(amountOfCakes: Int): List<Cake> {
    return reactiveOrder(amountOfCakes).await()
}
```

We can invoke this method using the following code:

```
fun main(args: Array<String>) = runBlocking {
    val cakes = Bakery().rxToCoroutinesOrder(10)
    println("Number of cakes: ${cakes.size}")
}
```

As you can see in the **Threads** pane, this code uses threads from an RxJava pool:

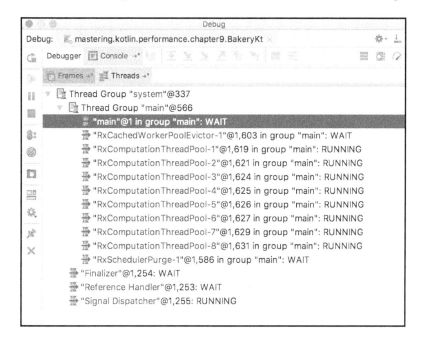

Summary

In this chapter, we looked at the use of coroutines and reactive programming. Using these approaches, you can write simple and reliable code that works in multithreaded environments. You can easily combine both styles in one project.

You can significantly increase the performance of your application using multithreading, but it can lead to a new class of asynchronous and synchronous issues in your project. You should avoid shared, mutable variables that are used across multiple threads and not forget about synchronization.

In the next chapter, we'll learn about best practices from the examples in this book.

10
Best Practices

This chapter offers a collection of best practices that we've discussed in this book. This collection is a set of rules or templates that you should follow in order to be able to write simple and reliable code without performance overhead.

We will cover the following topics in this chapter:

- The disposable pattern
- Immutability
- The String pool
- Functional programming
- Collections
- Properties
- Delegation
- Ranges
- Concurrency and parallelism

The disposable pattern

Use the disposable pattern along with the `try-finally` construction to avoid resource leaks.

 The **disposable pattern** is a pattern for resource management. This pattern assumes that an object represents a resource and that the resource can be released by invoking a method such as `close` or `dispose`.

The following example demonstrates how to use them:

```
fun readFirstLine() : String? {
    ......
    var bufferedReader: BufferedReader? = null
    return try {
        ......
        bufferedReader = BufferedReader(inputStreamReader)
        bufferedReader.readLine()
    } catch (e: Exception) {
        null
    } finally {
        ......
        bufferedReader?.close()
    }
}
```

The Kotlin standard library already has extension functions that use this approach under the hood:

```
fun readFirstLine(): String? = File("input.txt")
        .inputStream()
        .bufferedReader()
        .use { it.readLine() }
```

You should also remember the `dispose` method when you work with the `RxJava` library:

```
fun main(vars: Array<String>) {
    var memoryLeak: NoMemoryLeak? = NoMemoryLeak()
    memoryLeak?.start()
    memoryLeak?.disposable?.dispose()
    memoryLeak = NoMemoryLeak()
    memoryLeak.start()
    Thread.currentThread().join()
}

class NoMemoryLeak {

    init {
        objectNumber ++
    }

    private val currentObjectNumber = objectNumber

    var disposable: Disposable? = null

    fun start() {
        disposable = Observable.interval(1, TimeUnit.SECONDS)
```

```
                    .subscribe { println(currentObjectNumber) }
    }

    companion object {
        @JvmField
        var objectNumber = 0
    }
}
```

Immutability

If the state of an object can't be changed after it is initialized, then we consider this object immutable. **Immutability** allows you to write simple and reliable code. If the state of an object can't be changed, we can safely use it as a key for a map function, as in the following example:

```
fun main(vars: Array<String>) {
    data class ImmutableKey(val name: String? = null)
    val map = HashMap<ImmutableKey, Int>()
    map[ImmutableKey("someName")] = 2
    print(map[ImmutableKey("someName")])
}
```

We can consider the ImmutableKey class immutable because all its variables are marked with the val keyword and are initialized using a primary constructor.

Another significant thing about this example is that the ImmutableKey class is marked with the data modifier.

Data classes

Let's decompile our ImmutableKey to Java. The first lines look as follows:

```
final class ImmutableKey {
    @Nullable
    private final String name;

    @Nullable
    public final String getName() {
        return this.name;
    }

    public ImmutableKey(@Nullable String name) {
```

```
        this.name = name;
    }
```

. . . .

In the preceding snippet, we can see that the ImmutableKey class contains the name field with a getter and a constructor. The name field is marked with the final modifier; thus, it's initialized when a new instance is created, and after this, its value can't be changed.

The decompiled ImmutableKey also overrides a version of the toString method:

```
public String toString() {
    return "ImmutableKey(name=" + this.name + ")";
}
```

The ImmutableKey method also overrides the hashCode and equals methods:

```
public int hashCode() {
    return this.name != null ? this.name.hashCode() : 0;
}

public boolean equals(Object var1) {
    if (this != var1) {
        if (var1 instanceof ImmutableKey) {
            ImmutableKey var2 = (ImmutableKey)var1;
            if (Intrinsics.areEqual(this.name, var2.name)) {
                return true;
            }
        }

        return false;
    } else {
        return true;
    }
}
```

Classes that are marked with the data modifier override the hashCode and equals methods, hence data classes is an extremely powerful feature of Kotlin. All arguments from a primary constructor are used with these overridden methods. This feature allows you to reduce the amount of boilerplate code and avoid cases of typos. In the following code snippet, we use this feature in an example with a map function. The get method of the HashMap class uses the hashCode and equals methods of the key variable to find a value:

```
public V get(Object key) {
    Node<K,V> e;
```

```
        return (e = getNode(hash(key), key)) == null ? null : e.value;
    }
```

The `getNode` method looks as follows:

```
final Node<K,V> getNode(int hash, Object key) {
    Node<K,V>[] tab; Node<K,V> first, e; int n; K k;
    if ((tab = table) != null && (n = tab.length) > 0 &&
        (first = tab[(n - 1) & hash]) != null) {
        if (first.hash == hash && // always check first node
            ((k = first.key) == key || (key != null && key.equals(k))))
            return first;
        if ((e = first.next) != null) {
            if (first instanceof TreeNode)
                return ((TreeNode<K,V>)first).getTreeNode(hash, key);
            do {
                if (e.hash == hash &&
                    ((k = e.key) == key || (key != null && key.equals(k))))
                    return e;
            } while ((e = e.next) != null);
        }
    }
    return null;
}
```

The decompiled `ImmutableKey` class also contains the `copy` method:

```
@NotNull
public final ImmutableKey copy(@Nullable String name) {
    return new ImmutableKey(name);
}
```

The `copy` method is useful when we work with immutable objects. It allows us to create a new instance of an existing object with the same state or lets us pass parameters and have fields of a created object contain relevant values. Let's consider the following example:

```
fun main(vars: Array<String>) {
    data class ImmutableKey(val name: String? = null)
    val key = ImmutableKey()
    val copiedKey = key.copy()
    val copiedKeyWithAnotherName = key.copy(name = "AnotherName")
    println(key === copiedKey)
    println(key === copiedKeyWithAnotherName)
    println(key == copiedKey)
```

```
            println(key == copiedKeyWithAnotherName)
    }
```

The output shows that the `copy` method returns a reference to a newly created object:

```
false
false
true
false
```

If we pass parameters to the `copy` method, a newly created object will contain fields with values from these parameters. Otherwise, the result of comparing using the == operator or the `equals` method will be `true`. It's good practice to use immutable data classes when working with `map`s or `set`s, or when working in a multithreaded environment.

The String pool

If you create a string using quotes, the newly created object is automatically placed in a String pool. The String pool is a special section in memory that stores a set of unique strings. Whenever you create a new instance of the `String` class using quotes, the virtual machine looks for an equal string in the String pool and returns the found instance (if an instance exists). If an equal object isn't found, then a new instance is placed in the String pool before returning a reference to it. If you receive a new string from the outside, as in the following example, you can use the `intern()` method to push a string value to the String pool:

```
val firstLine: String
    get() = File("input.txt")
            .inputStream()
            .bufferedReader()
            .use { it.readLine() }
```

The following example shows that whenever you read the `firstLine` property, it returns a new instance of the `String` class:

```
fun main(vars: Array<String>) {
    println(firstLine === firstLine)
}
```

Let's have a look at the following output:

false

In some cases, for instance, if you read the `firstLine` property several times and compare it, you can improve its performance by using the `intern()` method:

```
fun main(vars: Array<String>) {
    println(firstLine.intern() === firstLine.intern())
}
```

Here's the output:

true

Remember that comparing by reference takes less time than comparing using the `equals` method.

StringBuilder

Strings are immutable, and whenever you try to modify an existing object, a new instance of the `String` class is created. The following example demonstrates this:

```
fun main(vars: Array<String>) {
    val cat1 = "Cat"
    val cat2 = cat1.plus("Dog")
    println(cat1)
    println(cat2)
    println(cat1 === cat2)
    println(cat1 === cat1)
}
```

Here's the output:

Cat
CatDog
false
true

So it's bad practice to use concatenation:

```
val query = "SELECT id, firstName, lastName FROM Building " + building + "
WHERE firstName = " + user.firstName
```

Instead, you should use the string templates feature:

```
val query = "SELECT id, firstName, lastName FROM Building $building WHERE
firstName = ${user.firstName}"
```

Under the hood, the string templates feature uses the `StringBuilder` class. We can check this using the Kotlin Bytecode inspector:

```
(new StringBuilder()).append("SELECT id, firstName, lastName FROM Building
").append(building).append(" WHERE firstName =
").append(user.getFirstName()).toString();
```

The `StringBuilder` class represents a mutable sequence of characters. It's not safe to use an instance of this class across several threads. In a multithread environment, we should use the `StringBuffer` class, which has similar public methods.

Functional programming

This section aims to consolidate your understanding of functional programming and when you should use it.

Functional programming is based on the following features:

- Pure functions
- First-class functions
- Higher-order functions
- Function composition
- Typeclasses
- Lambdas
- Closures
- Immutability

Contrary to object-oriented languages, which are written in an imperative style, functional programming languages are written in a declarative style.

Declarative versus imperative

With functional programming, you can write code that allows you to concentrate on business logic instead of specific implementations. The following example is written in an imperative style:

```
val numbers = listOf(1, 2, 3, 4, 5, 6, 7)
val odds = ArrayList<Int>()
for (i in 0..numbers.lastIndex) {
    val item = numbers[i]
    if (item % 2 != 0) {
        odds.add(item)
    }
}
```

If we rewrite this code in a declarative style, it will look as follows:

```
val numbers = listOf(1, 2, 3, 4, 5, 6, 7)
val odds = numbers.filter { it % 2 != 0 }
```

This code describes what it does instead of how it does it, making it easier to concentrate on the main logic of the application.

Pure functions

It's good practice to write code using **pure functions**. The results of these functions depend on parameters. Using this approach, you can write simple, reliable, and predictable code that's easy to test. Pure functions don't use any shared states, which is why they're safe to use in a multithreaded environment. The functions in the kotlin.math package are good examples of pure functions:

```
val minResult = min(3, 4)
val sqrtResult = sqrt(9.0)
```

First-class functions

If a function doesn't depend on the state of an object, you should declare it as a first-class citizen. For instance, the main function that we use as the starting point of every program is first-class. To create this function, you need to just declare it in the file as follows:

```
fun main(vars: Array<String>) {}
```

All pure functions can be declared in a similar way, for example, the `min` and `max` functions:

```
public inline fun min(a: Int, b: Int): Int = nativeMath.min(a, b)

public inline fun max(a: Int, b: Int): Int = nativeMath.max(a, b)
```

They delegate implementation to functions of a specific platform. In our case, it's `java.lang.Math`:

```
import java.lang.Math as nativeMath
```

But the `min` and `max` functions are first-class citizens.

If a function depends on the state of an object, this function is a method and should be declared as a class member. For instance, the `start` method of the `MemoryLeak` class depends on the `currentObjectNumber` property:

```
fun start() {
    Observable.interval(1, TimeUnit.SECONDS)
            .subscribe { println(currentObjectNumber) }
}
```

Higher-order functions

Higher-order functions are an extremely powerful way to reuse behavior flexibly. It's easy to implement the strategy pattern using higher-order functions.

Let's recall a good old example with compression that includes the `CompressionStrategy` interface:

```
public interface CompressionStrategy {
    File compress(File original);
}
```

Here's one implementation of this interface:

```
public class ZipCompressionStrategy implements CompressionStrategy {
    @Override
    public File compress(File original) {
        throw new NotImplementedException();
    }
}
```

And the `Archiver` class that holds a certain strategy and archives a file:

```
public class Archiver {
    private CompressionStrategy strategy;

    public CompressionStrategy getStrategy() {
        return strategy;
    }

    public void setStrategy(CompressionStrategy strategy) {
        this.strategy = strategy;
    }
    public File archive(File file) {
        return strategy.compress(file);
    }
}
```

Using features of Kotlin, we can implement this pattern in a single line of code:

```
inline fun File.archive(strategy: () -> File): File = strategy()
```

We can use this code as follows:

```
File("input.txt").archive { TODO() }.also {
    // do something with an archived file
}
```

Inline functions

Although Koltin is a modern programming language that has many features of functional programming, you should remember that it compiles to the same bytecode as Java. That's why it's good practice to use the Kotlin Bytecode inspector to check how your code works under the hood. When you work with higher-order functions, in most cases, you should use the `inline` modifier. Let's inspect the `Archive.kt` file.

When we use the `inline` modifier, we can see that the lambda code that we pass to the `archive` function is used directly in place of invocation:

```
public static final void main(@NotNull String[] args) {
    Intrinsics.checkParameterIsNotNull(args, "args");
    new File("input.txt");
    throw (Throwable)(new NotImplementedError((String)null, 1,
(DefaultConstructorMarker)null));
}
```

If we had written the `archive` function without the `inline` modifier, the extra class would have been generated with the following signature:

```
final class
mastering/kotlin/performance/chapter10/higher_order_function/ArchiverKt$mai
n$1 extends kotlin/jvm/internal/Lambda  implements
kotlin/jvm/functions/Function0  {
```

This class has three extra methods:

- `public synthetic bridge invoke()Ljava/lang/Object`
- `public final invoke()Ljava/lang/Void`
- `<init>()V`

In the version that has been decompiled to Java, we can see that an instance of this class is created and passed to the `archive` function:

```
@NotNull
public static final File archive(@NotNull File $receiver, @NotNull
Function0 strategy) {
    Intrinsics.checkParameterIsNotNull($receiver, "$receiver");
    Intrinsics.checkParameterIsNotNull(strategy, "strategy");
    return (File)strategy.invoke();
}

public static final void main(@NotNull String[] args) {
    Intrinsics.checkParameterIsNotNull(args, "args");
    File var1 = archive(new File("input.txt"), (Function0)null.INSTANCE);
}
```

You should use the inline modifier in most cases to prevent the creation of extra classes, objects, and methods.

Function composition

Function composition is a feature of functional programming that allows you to write simple and reliable code with significant performance improvements as compared with chain of function's invocations.

To avoid code such as this:

```
students
        .filter(::ageMoreThan20)
        .filter(::firstNameStartsWithE)
        .filter(::theLengthOfSecondNameMoreThan5)
```

You can write something like this:

```
fun predicate(student: Student)
        = ageMoreThan20(student)
        && firstNameStartsWithE(student)
        && theLengthOfSecondNameMoreThan5(student)

students.filter(::predicate)
```

Or you can create your function to implement function composition. This function may look like this:

```
inline infix fun <P> ((P) -> Boolean).and(crossinline predicate: (P) ->
Boolean): (P) -> Boolean {
    return { p: P -> this(p) && predicate(p) }
}
```

The preceding code snippet contains the `infix` function, which can be used as follows:

```
students
    .filter(::ageMoreThan20 and ::firstNameStartsWithE and
::theLengthOfSecondNameMoreThan5)
```

Or you can write a function like this:

```
inline operator fun <P1, R1, R2> ((R1) -> R2).plus(crossinline f: (P1) ->
R1): (P1) -> R2 {
    return { p1: P1 -> this(f(p1)) }
}
```

And change the sequence of the `map` methods:

```
return prices
        .map(::discount)
        .map(::tax)
        .map(::aid)
        .sum()
```

To something like this:

```
return prices
        .map(::aid + ::tax + ::discount)
        .sum()
```

Capturing lambdas

Capturing lambdas is a really convenient feature of Kotlin that allows you to write code like this:

```
fun main(args: Array<String>) {
    var counter = 0
    val inc = {
        counter ++
    }
    inc()
}
```

In the preceding snippet, a lambda changes a local variable of the main function. In Java, we can't do this because local variables are root objects for the garbage collector and we have to use some tricks to work around this. But it works in Kotlin out of the box. Decompiled to Java, this code looks like this:

```
public static final void main(@NotNull String[] args) {
    Intrinsics.checkParameterIsNotNull(args, "args");
    final IntRef counter = new IntRef();
    counter.element = 0;
    Function0 inc = (Function0)(new Function0() {
        // $FF: synthetic method
        // $FF: bridge method
        public Object invoke() {
            return this.invoke();
        }

        public final int invoke() {
            int var1 = counter.element++;
            return var1;
        }
    });
    inc.invoke();
}
```

As you can see, whenever you use capturing lambdas, extra objects and methods are created. Therefore, you should consider other options before using the capturing lambdas approach.

Collections

Always prefer read-only view collections over mutable ones. Since read-only view collections can't be changed, you can prevent a lot of bugs that relate to multithreading and state inconsistency. If you need to iterate elements of an `ArrayList`, consider the `while` loop:

```
inline fun <reified T> List<T>.foreach(crossinline invoke: (T) -> Unit):
Unit {
    val size = size
    var i = 0
    while (i < size) {
        invoke(get(i))
        i ++
    }
}
```

Sequences can improve performance significantly, especially if you use methods such as `first`:

```
@Benchmark
fun sequence() = (0..1_000_000)
        .asSequence()
        .filter { it % 2 == 0 }
        .map { it * it }
        .first()
```

Properties

To write code with minimum overhead, you first have to understand the difference between fields and properties. A **field** is just a variable of the class that holds a value. A **property** of the class includes the field, getter, and setter. Since Kotlin uses the concept of properties, you should know how to access a field directly without invoking the getter or setter.

Backing properties

If you need to access a field of a property inside a class in which it's declared, you can use backing properties. If you only need to access a field from the getter or setter of its property, it's enough to use backing fields. However, if you want to access a field somewhere else, you should use backing properties. Let's look at the following example:

```
class Button {
    private var _text: String? = null
    var text: String
        set(value) {
            println(value)
            _text = value
        }
        get() {
            return _text + _text
        }

    fun printText() {
        println(_text)
    }
}
```

In the preceding snippet, the _text variable is a field of the text property. To make sure of this, you can use the Kotlin Bytecode inspector:

```
public final class Button {
    private String _text;

    @NotNull
    public final String getText() {
        return Intrinsics.stringPlus(this._text, this._text);
    }

    public final void setText(@NotNull String value) {
        Intrinsics.checkParameterIsNotNull(value, "value");
        System.out.println(value);
        this._text = value;
    }

    public final void printText() {
        String var1 = this._text;
        System.out.println(var1);
    }
}
```

As you can see, the `printText` method uses a field of the `text` property directly without invoking a getter or setter. This approach can improve performance significantly if you run your program in a virtual machine that doesn't inline access fields.

@JvmField annotation

If you want to declare just a field with the `public` modifier and without a getter and setter, you can use the `@JvmField` annotation. In this case, we should follow the concept of object-oriented programming and encapsulate data and operations. But sometimes, we need a simple class such as `Point`, which can be used as follows:

```
val point = Point(3, 4)
point.x = 10
```

A naive approach in Kotlin is to create a class like this:

```
class Point(var x: Int, var y: Int)
```

If you decompile this class to Java, you'll see something like this:

```java
public final class Point {
    private int x;
    private int y;
    public final int getX() {
        return this.x;
    }
    public final void setX(int var1) {
        this.x = var1;
    }
    public final int getY() {
        return this.y;
    }
    public final void setY(int var1) {
        this.y = var1;
    }
    public Point(int x, int y) {
        this.x = x;
        this.y = y;
    }
}
```

The x and y variables are properties of the `Point` class, and they have fields, getters, and setters. We can use the `@JvmField` annotation to tell the compiler that we want to use these variables as fields, but not as properties:

```
class Point(@JvmField var x: Int, @JvmField var y: Int)
```

This code, when decompiled to Java, looks as follows:

```
public final class Point {
    @JvmField
    public int x;
    @JvmField
    public int y;

    public Point(int x, int y) {
        this.x = x;
        this.y = y;
    }
}
```

The `@JvmField` annotation can also be used to prevent the overhead of invoking getters and setters.

Top-level members

In Kotlin, we can declare variables and methods as top-level members, but not inside a class body. Let's look at the following example:

```
const val compileTime: Int = 5
fun compileTimeFunction() = compileTime + compileTime
```

This code, when decompiled to Java, looks as follows:

```
public final class MainKt {
    public static final int compileTime = 5;

    public static final int compileTimeFunction() {
        return 10;
    }
}
```

There's no overhead here. The `MainKt` class just contains two static members without `<cinit>()V` or static `<clinit>()V` methods. This is because we use the `const` modifier.

Compile-time constants

The `const` modifier allows you to declare **compile-time constants**. We can remove this modifier from our example and the version decompiled to Java will look as follows:

```
public final class MainKt {
    private static final int compileTime = 5;

    public static final int getCompileTime() {
        return compileTime;
    }

    public static final int compileTimeFunction() {
        return compileTime + compileTime;
    }
}
```

As you can see, now the `MainKt` class contains the extra `getCompileTime()` function. In the bytecode, you can see that the `MainKt` class also contains the `static <clinit>()V` function:

```
static <clinit>()V
L0
LINENUMBER 3 L0
ICONST_5
PUTSTATIC
mastering/kotlin/performance/chapter6/constants/MainKt.compileTime : I
RETURN
MAXSTACK = 1
MAXLOCALS = 0
```

You can use the `const` modifier with all types that can be decompiled to primitive Java and strings types. You can improve performance significantly using compile-time constants. Avoid variables that can't be compile-time constants. Let's add the `point` variable to our example:

```
val point = Point()
```

This code, when decompiled to Java, looks as follows:

```
public final class MainKt {
    @NotNull
    private static final Point point = new Point(0, 0, 3,
(DefaultConstructorMarker)null);
    public static final int compileTime = 5;

    @NotNull
```

```
    public static final Point getPoint() {
        return point;
    }

    public static final int compileTimeFunction() {
        return 10;
    }
}
```

The `MainKt` class contains the `static <clinit>()V` method.

The lateinit modifier

The `lateinit` modifier allows you to declare non-nullable variables without initializing them. Let's look at the following example:

```
class Main {
    private lateinit var name: String
    fun onCreate() {
        name = "Jack"
        println(name)
    }
}
```

This code, when decompiled to Java, looks as follows:

```
public final class Main {
    private String name;

    public final void onCreate() {
        this.name = "Jack";
        String var10000 = this.name;
        if (this.name == null) {
            Intrinsics.throwUninitializedPropertyAccessException("name");
        }

        String var1 = var10000;
        System.out.println(var1);
    }
}
```

Whenever you try to get a value from the `name` property, an additional check is invoked:

```
if (this.name == null) {
    Intrinsics.throwUninitializedPropertyAccessException("name");
}
```

It's better to assign a value from the `lateinit` property to a local variable:

```
fun onCreate() {
    name = "Jack"
    val name = this.name
    println(name)
    println(name)
}
```

This code, when decompiled to Java, looks as follows:

```
public final void onCreate() {
    this.name = "Jack";
    String var10000 = this.name;
    if (this.name == null) {
        Intrinsics.throwUninitializedPropertyAccessException("name");
    }

    String name = var10000;
    System.out.println(name);
    System.out.println(name);
}
```

As you can see, a check is only invoked once.

Delegation

Delegation is an extremely powerful feature of Kotlin. This section sums up several approaches that can improve the performance of your application.

Singleton delegate object

If you use `equals` objects as delegates several times, you can convert a delegate class to an object:

```
object CalculatorBrain: Calculator {
    override fun performOperation(operand: String): Int = TODO()
}
```

Then, you can use an instance of this class as a delegate object:

```
class CalculatorMachine(): Calculator by CalculatorBrain
```

Now, you don't need to create a new instance of the delegate object all the time and pass it to a constructor. You can also use a similar approach with delegated properties:

```
object SingletonDelegate : ReadOnlyProperty<Any?, String?> {
    override fun getValue(thisRef: Any?, property: KProperty<*>): String? {
        return property.name
    }
}
```

We can use `SingletonDelegate` as follows:

```
class Main {
    val property by SingletonDelegate
    val another by SingletonDelegate
}
```

The lazy funcation with unsafe thread mode

If you work in a single-thread environment, you can pass the `LazyThreadSafetyMode.NONE` object as a parameter:

```
private val rv by lazy(LazyThreadSafetyMode.NONE) {
    findViewById<RecyclerView>(R.id.rv)
}
```

Using this approach lets you avoid redundant checks and synchronizations.

Delegate object with generic

If you're going to use a delegate object for delegating objects of different types, you should create a separate class for each primitive type. You can create a single delegate class with a generic like this:

```
class GenericDelegate<T> : ReadOnlyProperty<Any?, T?> {
    override fun getValue(thisRef: Any?, property: KProperty<*>): T? {
        TODO()
    }
}
```

And use it as follows:

```
class Main {
    val property by GenericDelegate<Int>()
```

```
    val another by GenericDelegate<Float>()
}
```

But in this case, the getValue() method of the delegate object will return an instance of the Object type, and a cast to your generic type will occur:

```
@Nullable
  public final Integer getProperty() {
      return (Integer)this.property$delegate.getValue(this,
$$delegatedProperties[0]);
  }

  @Nullable
  public final Float getAnother() {
      return (Float)this.another$delegate.getValue(this,
$$delegatedProperties[1]);
  }
```

It's good practice to create a separate class for each primitive type. The IntDelegate class can look as follows:

```
class IntDelegate : ReadOnlyProperty<Any?, Int?> {
    override fun getValue(thisRef: Any?, property: KProperty<*>): Int? {
        TODO()
    }
}
```

And you can use it like this:

```
class Main {
    val property by IntDelegate()
    val another by GenericDelegate<Float>()
}
```

Ranges

Don't use nullable types with ranges. Let's look at the following example:

```
fun main(args: Array<String>) {
    val int = args[0].toInt()
    if (int in 0..10) {
        println(int)
    }
}
```

This code, when decompiled to Java, looks as follows:

```java
public static final void main(@NotNull String[] args) {
   Intrinsics.checkParameterIsNotNull(args, "args");
   String var2 = args[0];
   int value = Integer.parseInt(var2);
   if (0 <= value) {
      if (10 >= value) {
         System.out.println(value);
      }
   }
}
```

As you can see, there's no overhead here. But if we use a nullable integer:

```kotlin
fun main(args: Array<String>) {
   val value = args[0].toIntOrNull()
   if (value in 0..10) {
       println(value)
   }
}
```

Then this code, when decompiled to Java, looks as follows:

```java
public static final void main(@NotNull String[] args) {
   Intrinsics.checkParameterIsNotNull(args, "args");
   Integer value = StringsKt.toIntOrNull(args[0]);
   byte var2 = 0;
   if (CollectionsKt.contains((Iterable)(new IntRange(var2, 10)), value)) {
      System.out.println(value);
   }
}
```

Another example relates to the when expression. Let's look at the following common example:

```kotlin
val value = args[0].toInt()
when(value) {
    in 100..200 -> println("Informational responses")
    in 200..300 -> println("Success")
    in 300..400 -> println("Redirection")
    in 400..500 -> println("Client error")
    in 500..600 -> println("Server error")
}
```

The decompiled version looks like this:

```
String var2 = args[0];
int value = Integer.parseInt(var2);
String var3;
if (100 <= value) {
    if (200 >= value) {
        var3 = "Informational responses";
        System.out.println(var3);
        return;
    }
}

if (200 <= value) {
    if (300 >= value) {
        var3 = "Success";
        System.out.println(var3);
        return;
    }
}
..........
```

As you can see, there's no overhead here. But if we use a nullable type:

```
val value = args[0].toIntOrNull()
```

Then this code, when decompiled to Java, looks as follows:

```
Integer value = StringsKt.toIntOrNull(args[0]);
byte var3 = 100;
String var4;
if (CollectionsKt.contains((Iterable)(new IntRange(var3, 200)), value)) {
    var4 = "Informational responses";
    System.out.println(var4);
} else {
    short var5 = 200;
    if (CollectionsKt.contains((Iterable)(new IntRange(var5, 300)), value))
{
        var4 = "Success";
        System.out.println(var4);
    } else {
        var5 = 300;
..................
```

You should also use a single type in ranges. Let's look at the following example:

```
val value = args[0].toLong()
when(value) {
    in 100L..200L -> println("Informational responses")
    in 200L..300L -> println("Success")
    in 300L..400L -> println("Redirection")
    in 400.0..500.0 -> println("Client error")
    in 500.0..600.0 -> println("Server error")
}
```

The last two ranges use the Double type, but we check a value of the Long type. The decompiled version looks like this:

```
String var3 = args[0];
long value = Long.parseLong(var3);
String var5;
if (100L <= value) {
    if (200L >= value) {
        var5 = "Informational responses";
        System.out.println(var5);
        return;
    }
}

. . . . . . . . . . . . . . .

if (RangesKt.doubleRangeContains((ClosedRange)RangesKt.rangeTo(400.0D,
500.0D), value)) {
    var5 = "Client error";
    System.out.println(var5);
} else if
(RangesKt.doubleRangeContains((ClosedRange)RangesKt.rangeTo(500.0D,
600.0D), value)) {
    var5 = "Server error";
    System.out.println(var5);
}
```

If you have a loop with a break condition, such as the first() method, use the asSequence() method. The benchmark that looks as follows:

```
@Benchmark
fun rangeSequenceLoop(blackhole: Blackhole)
        = range.asSequence()
            .map { it * 2 }
            .first { it % 2 == 0 }
```

Is much faster than this one:

```
@Benchmark
fun rangeLoop(blackhole: Blackhole)
        = range
            .map { it * 2 }
            .first { it % 2 == 0 }
```

Concurrency and parallelism

You should use special approaches to deal with multithreading, such as RxJava or coroutines. Using RxJava, you can easily process asynchronous events in several threads:

```
fun singleBake(): Single<Cake> {
    return Single.fromCallable { bake()
}.subscribeOn(Schedulers.computation())
}

fun reactiveOrder(amountOfCakes: Int): Single<List<Cake>> {
    val baker = Baker()
    return Observable.range(0, amountOfCakes)
            .flatMapSingle { baker.singleBake() }
            .toList()
}

.....................

Bakery().reactiveOrder(10)
  .subscribe { cakes -> println("Number of cakes: ${cakes.size}")}
```

Use common patterns to synchronize the work of several threads:

```
val lock = Lock()

Bakery().reactiveOrder(10)
        .doAfterTerminate { lock.unlock() }
        .subscribe { cakes ->  println("Number of cakes: ${cakes.size}")}

lock.lock()
```

You can use coroutines to write asynchronous code in a sequential style:

```
suspend fun coroutinesOrder(amountOfCakes: Int): List<Cake> {
    val baker = Baker()
    return (0 until amountOfCakes)
            .map { async { baker.bake() } }
            .map { it.await()}
}

fun main(args: Array<String>) = runBlocking {
    val cakes = Bakery().coroutinesOrder(10)
    println("Number of cakes: ${cakes.size}")
}
```

If you want to integrate coroutines in an application that already contains the RxJava library, you don't need to rewrite code. You can use a library such as kotlinx-coroutines-rx2 (https://github.com/Kotlin/kotlinx.coroutines/tree/master/reactive/kotlinx-coroutines-rx2) to convert live collections of the RxJava library to coroutines, and vice versa.

You should use patterns like *actor* to avoid a shared, mutable state in a multithreaded environment. The actor pattern is based on sending messages like this:

```
sealed class CounterMsg
object IncCounter : CounterMsg()
class GetCounter(val response: CompletableDeferred<Int>) : CounterMsg()
```

To an actor that handles these messages as follows:

```
fun counterActor() = actor<CounterMsg> {
    var counter = 0
    for (msg in channel) {
        when (msg) {
            is IncCounter -> counter++
            is GetCounter -> msg.response.complete(counter)
        }
    }
}
```

The massiveRun function just invokes an action:

```
suspend fun massiveRun(context: CoroutineContext, action: suspend () ->
Unit) {
    val n = 1000
    val k = 1000
    val time = measureTimeMillis {
        val jobs = List(n) {
```

```
        launch(context) {
            repeat(k) { action() }
        }
    }
    jobs.forEach { it.join() }
}
println("Completed ${n * k} actions in $time ms")
}
```

You can use the actor pattern as follows:

```
fun main(args: Array<String>) = runBlocking<Unit> {
    val counter = counterActor()
    massiveRun(CommonPool) {
        counter.send(IncCounter)
    }
    val response = CompletableDeferred<Int>()
    counter.send(GetCounter(response))
    println("Counter = ${response.await()}")
    counter.close()
}
```

Summary

In this chapter, we've summed up all of the previous chapters and listed their best practices in order to create robust applications with high performance. Now you know how to use the disposable and actor patterns and how to inspect and debug Kotlin code. You've acquired some expertise in writing benchmarks and inspecting bytecode and you now understand that Kotlin is a modern and powerful programming language that's designed to interoperate with Java. You know that you should use the Kotlin Bytecode inspector and other profiling tools to write high-performance code.

Thank you for taking your time to read this book and I wish you the best of luck.

Other Books You May Enjoy

If you enjoyed this book, you may be interested in these other books by Packt:

Hands-On Microservices with Kotlin
Juan Antonio Medina Iglesias

ISBN: 978-1-78847-145-9

- Understand microservice architectures and principles
- Build microservices in Kotlin using Spring Boot 2.0 and Spring Framework 5.0
- Create reactive microservices that perform non-blocking operations with Spring WebFlux
- Use Spring Data to get data reactively from MongoDB
- Test effectively with JUnit and Kotlin
- Create cloud-native microservices with Spring Cloud
- Build and publish Docker images of your microservices
- Scaling microservices with Docker Swarm
- Monitor microservices with JMX
- Deploy microservices in OpenShift Online

Functional Kotlin

Mario Arias, Rivu Chakraborty

ISBN: 978-1-78847-648-5

- Learn the Concepts of Functional Programming with Kotlin
- Discover the Coroutines in Kotlin
- Uncover Using funkTionale plugin
- Learn Monads, Functiors and Applicatives
- Combine Functional Programming with OOP and Reactive Programming
- Uncover Using Monads with funkTionale
- Discover Stream Processing

Leave a review - let other readers know what you think

Please share your thoughts on this book with others by leaving a review on the site that you bought it from. If you purchased the book from Amazon, please leave us an honest review on this book's Amazon page. This is vital so that other potential readers can see and use your unbiased opinion to make purchasing decisions, we can understand what our customers think about our products, and our authors can see your feedback on the title that they have worked with Packt to create. It will only take a few minutes of your time, but is valuable to other potential customers, our authors, and Packt. Thank you!

Index

R

Random Access Memory (RAM) 26
ranges
  about 287, 288, 290
  benchmarking 227, 228, 229, 231, 233, 234
  in Kotlin 211, 213, 214, 216, 218, 220, 222
  utility functions 224, 225, 226
reactive programming
  about 241
  example 241, 243, 245, 246, 247, 248, 249,
    250, 251, 252, 253
resource leaks 15

S

sequences
  in Kotlin 145
sets
  about 132
  operations 132
  time complexity 139
singleton delegate object 285
slow rendering
  about 31
  device refresh rate 31
  frame rate 32
stack 130, 131
String pool 23, 270, 271
String Templates
  reference 25
StringBuilder 271
suspendingSequence function 260
synchronization 30

T

thread profiling, in MAT
  about 85
  Thread Details pane 86
  Threads Overview pane 85
threads profiling 81
Threads viewer
  about 82
  Frame pane 83
  Threads pane 84
time complexity
  about 137
  calculating 138
  of lists 139
  of maps 140
  of queues 140
  of sets 139
TimeUnit enum
  reference 18
top-level members 282
tries 135
typeclasses
  about 105
  Arrow library 105
  Functor 106, 107
  Monad 109, 111

U

unanticipated delegation 186
undirected graph 137
user interface rendering 33

V

vertices 137